Lucas Myer

West: A Translation

ALSO BY PAISLEY REKDAL

West: A Translation
Paisley Rekdal

COPPER CANYON PRESS
PORT TOWNSEND, WASHINGTON

Cover artwork: *Winslow, Arizona. A young Indian laborer working in the Atchison, Topeka and Santa Fe Railroad yard,* Farm Security Administration/Office of War Information Collection, Library of Congress.

Copper Canyon Press is in residence at Fort Worden State Park in Port Townsend, Washington, under the auspices of Centrum. Centrum is a gathering place for artists and creative thinkers from around the world, students of all ages and backgrounds, and audiences seeking extraordinary cultural enrichment.

The Library of Congress has catalogued this record under LCCN 2022047265.

9 8 7 6 5 4 3 2 FIRST PRINTING

COPPER CANYON PRESS
Post Office Box 271
Port Townsend, Washington 98368
www.coppercanyonpress.org

IN MEMORIAM JUDGE MICHAEL WEI KWAN (1962–2020)
AND CORKY LEE (1947–2021).

Notes   11/6/23

- wanted to find cultural significance

- Translated through lense of the railroad

- Transcontinental and chinese exclusion

- Reads as it looks (captures rythym of train)
  ↳ poem dead

Journey: built because of golden spike.
          ↳ Old trainwrecks

Regret p. 54 —
          ↳ took notes
          ↳ Black women treated worse

Hold sorrow: prostitution & took notes on page

Presidential
impeachment: Parallels between now and then.
          ↳ Compared Trump and Johnson
          ↳ Reads Johnson then Trump. Racism - Very racist, saw
          land for white people

Trump: Begins to speak about immigration.
  ↳ Reads them together. Gives them
  a single voice. Makes them the same.

Chinese Death rituals:
  Body: always returned home (sent back to China)
  Not written by her. Directly from Newspaper articles
  ↳ Described railroad as human, but workers described
  as a machine

Return: Body goes back to homeland
Making country whole - then connected with bi-racial.

Not Ash: About bi-racial. Important to her as she is
  like her.
      ↳ Doesn't feel like they belong.
          ↳ Very deep. From Jamait lot perspective

          Q and A

  Titles are Incorrect translates

Wanted to translate characters in the most literal way
Wanted to create disconnect between languages
Always losing something while translating (History/tongue
Book plays with truth and accuracy.
Utopian history. Surprising to see that railroad was
act of conquest
Deliberately searched for peoples. Thinks a lot about
cultural appropriation.
Felt like DJ
  Make language physical material

It is impossible to grieve in the first-person singular.

CRISTINA RIVERA GARZA

Contents

West: A Translation

噩耗傳聞實可哀，
吊君何日裹屍回？
無能瞑目憑誰訴？
有識應知悔此來。
千古含愁千古恨，
思鄉空對望鄉臺。
未酬壯志埋壤土，
知爾雄心死不灰。

噩耗 / **Sorrowful News**

Sorrowful news sings the telegram
and Lincoln's body slides from DC
to Springfield, his third son, Willie,
boxed beside him. Buffalo,
Cleveland, Painesville, Ashtabula:
two coffins, 1,700 miles, 14 days
on 14 railroads. *One day a great line*
will unite us, the president promised.
Father and son conveyed
capital to capital. Lewisville,
New Albany, Baltimore, Chicago:
the black trains beach upon a tide of roses.
Can you believe still in the promise of this union?
I saw, General Dodge wrote, *a little negro*
drop on his knees and offer prayers,
while above, the dark news rang
on wires: *gone gone gone gone*
across telegraph poles tall as the gallows
from which the president
ordered 38 Dakota hanged.

4

傳 / **Pass**

Brigham Young hoped passing trains
would enliven trade, while Congress
hoped trade would pass polygamy
from existence. Stanford didn't think the Chinese
could pass muster, then used them to pass up
the Irish, after which he wanted Chinese out,
passed over by law to keep them from passing
for white. The work passed
to Japanese, who were put in camps, then on
to Mexicans, Navajo, Italians, Poles, Greeks, Swedes,
each man passed into and out of
some approximation of American. "We cannot fail
to be benefitted by it," wrote Brigham Young.
A bond paid down per mile
of track, Congress had to pass an act
to make the building stop. It's in the past,
but first these barons didn't plan
to meet: they planned to win. Each side
built right on past the other.

聞 / **Learn**

"To his Excellency Gov. Bigler," *Daily Alta California,*
5 May 1852

[handwritten: Format is cool]

Sir: I am a Chinaman, republican, lover
of these United
States. I have learned

of your recent   *[handwritten: broken english?]*

arguments to exclude
Chinese workers from entering

this State so as,
you say, to enhance
its wealth, a thought which forgets

population, too,
is wealth: that once you looked
for immigration

and it came, and made you great
throughout the nations
of the earth. I am sure

you will recognize your own
familial origins
in this story as

your Excellency, like all white men,
would never boast
of having a red man

for a father. I am sure
the Constitution does not admit
asylum only

6

to the pale face, even as it holds   — *alluding racism*
            the Negro here
    in forced servitude.

                                As far as the aristocracy
                    of skin is concerned, Sir,
                            ours compares

with the European
            races, though the framers
    of your declaration, I believe,

                                never argued for an aristocracy
                    of skin. Sir, we are as allied
                        to the African and red man

as you are.
            We must remind you
        that when your nation

                            was a wilderness,
                we exercised the arts
                    of commerce, science: we grew

a civilization while your own one   *ancient China*
            languished, helpless,
        in the dark.

                            We will not be reproved now
                for pursuing any work here
                    you consider degrading

to a man's character, or accept
            your condemnation except
        you consider labor

7

          degrading for itself.
      We, like you,
        make our own way

into the future.
      We have learned to trust
    in law's distinctions even

            as we daily see how law
        is bent here to fit
        a changing prejudice:

one day soon, such prejudice
      may benefit us.
    I hope you take this message, Sir,

          in all the spirit
      of candor. I have the honor to be,
      Norman Asing,

your Excellency's
    obedient servant—

實可 / **Indeed**

they look down with contempt
upon our newer   rougher civilization
they do not identify
with our country   their great care
is to be buried at home
though our demand for them daily
increases   we want 10,000
of them   we want 100,000   ~ Chinese immigrants
we want half
a million to bring the price
of labor down   there shall be
500 cubic feet of air
between them   restrictions
made upon their testimony
against white men   they shall not walk
on our sidewalks or marry
a white man or woman   all this
and they shall keep the Negro
steady   they are quiet
good cooks   good
at almost everything
they are put at   indeed
the only trouble is
we cannot talk to them ~ language

哀 / **Sad**

If he would stay in the White House, keep his mouth shut, and not make a fool of himself, disgusting friend and foe alike . . . the President of the United States might command some respect.

Potter County Journal, on Andrew Johnson's Swing Around the Circle
train tour, 1866

At this particular crisis
of the American people, I cling to the Constitution:
notwithstanding a mendacious press,
that common gang of cormorants and bloodsuckers,
the pains Congress has taken to malign
what all patriotic men should rally round:
there is no power that can control me.
Before I would see this Government destroyed
I would send every Negro back to Africa.
I will indeed be your Moses.
There are a good many people
but this is a country for white men,
hence you can see why I have been assaulted.
I hand over to you this flag, though imprisoned.
I feel confident you agree to the same great doctrine,
if these are your tender mercies, God,

We have shattered the mentality,
the broken promises, jobless recoveries, tired platitudes—
nobody has done anything like I've been able to do.
I alone can fix
that strong border. They want a wall,
that Chinese virus I call it because
when somebody is president of the US, that authority is total
to silence your voices on social media.
They're bringing drugs, they're bringing crimes. Sad!
And then you get into legal semantics
on both sides. So we had a campaign.
Sorry, women, thank you for that big victory!
It's called total acquittal and now
I am your voice. I view everybody as a threat,
except for possibly Abe Lincoln:
Trust me. There will be no lies.

吊 / **Lament**

Among the longest-
        lived creatures on earth, *sequoia*
sempervirens can exceed

        a fir's height by 200
feet, the base of its trunk
        wider than a horse carriage

or city lot. Its tallest example
        is named Hyperion, its largest
Grogan's Fault, discovered

        after 2,000 years of obscurity to all
but itself, this tree that feeds
        on fog, bears

both pollen and seed cone for self-
        insemination. It can churn through
humus and bedrock for burls to adopt

        as seedlings after fire, the awl-
shaped leaves—dark green, with blue-
        white bands of stomata—spire-

topped to trap each glimpse
        of sun. Richer than wine
with tannic acid, rilled

        with sapsucker pocks, the fluted
bark resists fungus, insect,
        damp, and rot. Flickers

and deer mice thrive
        within its branch wells.
So, too, do salamanders

and pseudoscorpions,
vines of huckleberry, tree frogs
and webworm moths,

the silver-haired bat and fringed
myotis. Named for the man
who developed the Cherokee

syllabary, this tree's
fire scars have housed
horse stables and itinerant

families inside their gouges, the milled
planks alone remaining
untouched when San Francisco

burned, these lovers
of flood and flame, that cannot conduct heat
and compensate for weakness

by sloughing and splitting,
buttressing wind-lean with selective
wood growth. Once covering,

in 1850, over 2 million acres,
they now prevail in strips and plots
totaling 40,000

football fields. Stanford,
attracted to what he saw
of their strength, ordered steam

engines into groves to drag logs down
through skid trails, the heartwood stacked
on railroad pallets to make

more railroad; billets
         uprooted, trekked, scattered
on the opposite coast where

         Charles Sheeler painted
Rolling Power, his portrait of Dreyfuss's
         Twentieth Century Limited,

the locomotive's wheel wells slick
         as cloisonné in olives,
grays, and browns.

         The most spectacular
American invention yet,
         Sheeler marveled, and painted

the buckskin ties tamped tight
         to their irons,
shadowing his canvas margin.

何日 / **What Day**

On this <u>seventh</u> day
of the s<u>even</u>th month, magpies
     bridge in a cluster
     of black and white

the Sky King crosses
to meet his Queen, time tracked
     by the close-knit wheeling
     of stars. <u>I watch.</u> You come

to me tonight, drunk on wine
and cards, nails ridged black
     with <u>opium</u>
     <u>to ease the pain</u>

of work. We are
all men here. Any
     body can be
     a bridge, little raven,

your eyes squeezed shut
but not from pain.
     We are
     a trestle, a grade

we build together.
<u>What matter if you say</u>
     you'd never choose
     me, were there

women willing
in this desert. I
     chose. I choose
     the memory we share

of rivers, your hair
of smoke and raw,
       wet leather. A man
       in another

man's hand makes himself
tool or weapon, says
       the overseer, as if a man's use
       to another is only one

of work. Pleasure
is our only chosen
       future. You
       are the home

I briefly make, the country
I can return to. Here
       where the moon wheels
       its white shoulder

in the dark as you push me
to the earth, slip
       my whiskered tip
       of hair into your mouth.

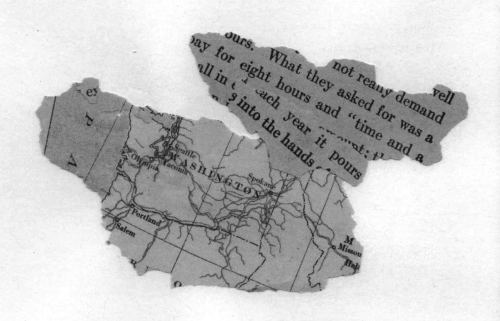

裏 / **Wrap**

Dear Margaret It is called Scarletteena the disorder

is all in the throat The boy I said

is a son of Henry's that lives with us

he has another James lives with his mother

this boy is about 8 years the other between 6 and 7

Dear Margaret I cannot find words to express

at all times in sickness in death Dear Margaret

We are sorry about your house being burned

we hope you have got another

Dear John

The shoemakers are on strike here

about 500 walking out. The masters

want to reduce them 20%

of the wages they had and the men

won't stand it. There is not

enough work here for the Blacks, let alone

white people. My mind is a hell to me.

There is about 100,000 idle here and every

ship brings out hundreds more.

If you know anybody that is thinking

of coming out tell them for God sake

stop where they are. I found Maurice

Murphy and he gave me 1 dollar

on Tuesday, Saint Patrick Day.

He has no work either. For God sake John

don't let anybody know the way we are off

nothing doing no

expectation, nothing to fall back on

in the way of trade, crops failed

these two or three year back, not much

provisions imported, exports limited

to deals, railroad Sleepers, Grinding

Stones, our square timber

is all consumed or at least

the forest is done, this Will

give an idea of our State at present

also of our future prospects

over the Blooming
the downing sun
first on the mink
of love and think
that I _____ for by and _____,

Dear Father Pen could not write the distress

of the Irish Passengers which arrived thro

Sickness death of every Kind

there are thousands of them buried

on the Island, let me know

how James Burns and Sister are let me know

how John Burns is, Biddy Kelly and family.

Milk and Butter is very dear here

write as soon as you can

I will be uneasy untill I hear from you

As I have a notion to marry

again if I could get

a Safe Match please Send

some good young widows or old

maids Its a fact weman

of all kinds are rather Scarce here but

Especially good ones. Pick out one

for me and tell her I will take her

on your reccomend and pay her passage

into the Bargain I am one year younger

than you and have two good Horses

4 cows 8 sheep 20 Hogs 80 Acres

timbered land about 30 of it

improved and all tools to work

my farm and am a carpenter to Boot

Markets rate as follows Potatoes 1s.3d. p stone Butter 1s. 3d. per Pound flower for 196
Pounds 35 shillings Eggs 8d.

interesting

—By the way how is Tommy

getting along tell him not to fall in love

with any yankey

hooker doodle

Dear Cousin: Maggie

has not had a letter from you

for ever and of course

I tell her that if I

was as long without a letter I

should be crazy really, Johnie,

you do not write, what is the trouble,

Good Night with love

from your cousin PS

You did well to hold onto your horse

do you remember, how did it get so wild

Edward McCarthy Dear Ned

You will think it strange of me to ask

as I already got one picture but the eyes

are so dull you can harly notice them

the man said if I could get the lend

of others he would try to paint

one right away, he is a splendid hand

his name is Frost bookkeeper.

I hope you wont refuse

the first favour I ask of you for the lend

of Jims picture now to paint

I am trying to have one

coppied it will be so nice for the children

to look at when we are dead

Dear wife

15 new cases + 9 deaths. Persons attacked

frequently do not live

more than 5 or 6 hours. If the Cholera

should increase I think I shall go

to Portland altho I suppose

I should lose my situation

dont let this alarm you.

I will write again tomorrow

or next day—give my love

to all the dear children perhaps

I ought not to have written as I have

Bye Bye Johnie

My health thank God

is pretty Good, my age

is pretty round I am wrestling

with Mr Sixty but I hope

I will get at the other Side

of him, I am Gray,

and I wear spectacles,

I am sober and I do not drink

I am well liked, and I offend no

body, and I am happy

to hear from you at all times

when you are pleased to write

We had strawberries & cream
coconut chocolate & biscuit,
lobster salad & coffee

Wrote a leter to John John and send him 5D,
Wrote some poetry

Said Mary to a frolicsome brook
That was running away

The crosseyed fellow came & the fox

I'm going to leave tomorrow forever

⌐ / **Body**

The pocket appeal will override the prejudices of his soul.
Samuel Bowles

A carload passed last night, their bones
returned in barrels marked "pickles." Thick
as bees, ants, locusts, Celestials
lay siege to Nature in her strongest
citadel. Their genius
is imitation; show them once
to do a thing, and their education
is complete. Wherever you put them,
you'll find them good. They can withstand
freezing, hunger, thirst, and heat; their simple,
narrow, but not dull minds running
in old grooves. Congealed quantities.
Crystals of social substance. Eunuchated
as boys or sodomites, they breed, defunct
in the heat of germs. They can be shipped
to shore in great quantities.
Even their clothes come, identical,
studded with rivets.

回 / **Return**

If falling leaves return to roots, what grows
when leaves cannot be gathered?
What returns if not the body? What remains
if not the soul? Who is to say these graves
empty of their bones mean only loss, not
that these men escaped death's hold entirely:
they are not home, but they are not here,
either, or have become so full of *here*
we need another word than *gone*. So throw
out the cormorant, its leg tied with silken ropes.
Let it drag the air for memory. Over and over,
as many times as you want. You can't snare
what isn't missing. This country claimed their bodies.
It never trapped their souls.

f snow and
s slid bodily

無 / Not

Speeches of Dennis Kearney, Labor Champion, 1878

I am not a railroad
king, banker, professor, bummer
politician. Under their flag

of slaveholder they
have rallied and we
permitted them to grow rich. They

have loaded down our nation
with debt. They
have stolen public lands; by their

unprincipled greed brought
distress on millions, they
who have resources enough to feed,

clothe, and shelter the entire
human race. We
propose now to take charge.

The press will say I
am a common
Irishman. Good. I am

a working man, too, like you,
who did not come here
as English, Scotch, Dutch, or Irish;

not Catholic, either, Protestant, or Infidel.
Let there be no sects.
We are white

working men who will elect
the hardfisted: obscure
artisans, coopers, bank-smashers. If

the legislature oversteps
human decency, then rope
will be our battle cry.

White men, women,
girls and boys will not compete
with the mechanics

of the market. The Chinese
must leave our shores. None
but an idiot would hope to work

as cheap; none but a slave
make the effort. Death
is preferable to life

on par with these. We
make no secret
of our intentions. We can discuss

if it would be better to hang,
shoot, or cut the capitalists to pieces
later. Money

is always on alert
to divide us. But as I walk
under this starless heaven,

still I know
Mars holds its course, Venus whirls
in flashing fields of light. Thus it is

with a movement
                of our kind. We
        are working men and we

                                will exhibit ourselves
                when the time is right. Not
                        in lowliness or in shame

but splendor: alive
                in the heart of our true
        and native powers.

能 / **Able**

A Chinese and English Phrase Book in the Canton Dialect, or
Dialogues on Ordinary and Familiar Subjects, 1888

Lesson XXIX

My name is Ah Quong.

I was cook for Mrs. Black on Tenth street for three years.

I can bring you good references.

I must answer the door-bell promptly.

I hear she wants a Chinese cook.

The men are striking for wages.

Can you put a bolt on this door for me?

Here is the ticket for your clothes.

Here are your folded shirts.

I am content with my situation.

When you wait on the table, Charley, you must wear a white apron.

Yes, this is our contract.

How much does it cost?

I don't know; I am a stranger here myself.

[Handwritten annotations: "1 sentence per line", "after a good amount of time still feels like a stranger / very patient?", "broken english", "railroad", "Helping", "I wonder who she", "Stranger in terms of immigration / Feels not at home", "Sounds like she might be someones paper mother or she is speaking to an immigrant"]

36

These children come from the best orphanages in and around New York and have been diligently trained and selected with care to fit the new family life into which they are to enter. If a mistake has been made in the choice, or for any reason the child be not satisfactory, the society bears the trouble and expense of its return by rail.

newspaper from Maquoketa, Iowa, 31 October 1919

瞑目 / **Close Eye**

When I was five a man
found me on my corner, asked
in German if I was hungry. And when
I told him yes he took my hand
and led me to Saint Dominic's where there
was bread and milk and sometimes meat, where there
was Daisy who snapped her fingers
in matron's face and said that she was sick
of looking after little
boys like me. She said it in

American but I was German
then and she was not
my mother she said but pushed
a sandwich for me anyway through the gate
and made me wear
a woolen cap that scratched my ears
and wrapped a ribbon through the tears
in my knees so my legs wore lines
of silk. And she held my hand
at the depot where they took us
and called me *little* to the others
on the train but I could hear the whispers
by our door each night
and feel the cold
hard knob of coins she knotted
in her skirt come morning. *Silver*
for the color of your mother's
eyes she sang as we crossed the plains
but I do not remember
what my mother ever looked like.

And she taught me a song
and she taught me a dance
and she taught me to speak a piece of poetry
to the farmers at the depot
where we were dropped and say
mother in American
if a woman ever looked at us and I thought
someone from the crowd would take us both
but one took her and Dan
took me and here I am

with the goats I learned to milk,
the heavy pail I do not spill, my mouth
full of words said the way they like them so
I never get the belt. I have a puppy here
and chores, all meals. The streets
are dirt and when it rains it comes as mud.
There are no crowds, no coins, no ribbons
at my knees. They were white
I remember as the stairs
I spend my Sundays
sweeping. There is a stain
I don't get out no matter if Dan helps me scrub.
You have to shut your eyes
to a lot of dirt out here, Dan winks
and touches my head
and sometimes calls me Son.

CHARLES LAWRENCE—German, sixteen years old, carries a little traveling bag in which he keeps a number of old newspapers he calls his library.

CHARLES MCGINN—Thirteen, his right father died when he was a month old, shot over in Jersey.

ANNIE RIGGS—This girl, age fifteen, is a Canadian who wishes to return to her family.

JOHN RILEY—An American, age twelve. Father was a Hod-carrier. Mother drinks a great deal.

MARY JANE SCOTT—Left her former place because they used to sew the children up in bags at night.

ANNA DALAGHAN—Twelve, this girl promises to be a fine woman.

EDGAR SPITTLER—Young baker by trade, who is left with two young brothers to be taken care of. An uncle in Hicksville, Ill., although a well-to-do farmer, will have nothing to do with them.

THOMAS WINTERLY—Said to possess considerable ability impersonating characters. Managed to support himself by peddling glassware.

J.H.—This boy is ten. Father dead, mother has been arrested. Has studied arithmetic as far as the cancellation of fractions.

FRED G. SOLLETT—Twelve, said to be an electrical genius.

R.G.—Age nine. Nothing could be learned of his former condition.

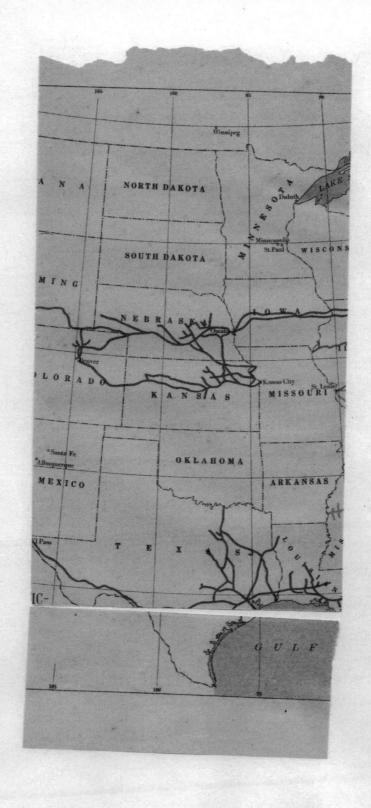

憑 / **To**

Ogden
Corinne
Promontory
Monument
Kelton
Mathie
Terrace
Lucia
Tecoona
Montello
Loray
Toano
Pequop
Independence
Wells
Tulasco
Halleck
Osino
Elko
Molem
Carlin
Beowawe
Shoshone
Argenta
Battle Mountain
Stone House
Golconda
Winnemucca
Raspberry
Mill City
Humboldt
Rye Patch

Oreana
Lovelock's
Brown's
White Plains
Hot Springs
Wadsworth
Clark's
Camp 37
Reno
Verdi
Boca
Truckee
Summit
Cisco
Emigrant Gap
Blue Canyon
Alta
Dutch Flat
Gold Run
Colfax
Auburn
Newcastle
Rocklin
Junction
Arcade
Sacramento

o'ippeh nemme kai tetseewai

Tan ko'ippeh nemme kai tetseewait

Tan ko'ippeh nemme kai tetseewaite

誰 / **Who**

Omaha
Pawnee
Lakota
Cheyenne
Arapaho
Ute
Shoshone
Goshute
Northern Paiute
Washoe
Maidu
Wintun
Miwok
Yokuts
Castano

訴 / **Tell**

A. Fleming, correspondent, *The Pittsburgh Commercial*,
25 August 1868

"Long tongue," Indians call
the telegraph and I'm told
superstition prevents
them cutting down the poles
or tearing up tracks whose irons
seem too warm to their unfamiliar
touch. All this I can report
to Pittsburgh's readers, though
the darkest tales, our handlers
warn, we must suppress.
I heard a doctor tell
of how he watched a Sioux
snatch an arrow from his own
split chest, shoot it back
at his half-breed
pursuer. I heard of women
scalped alive, of Sherman's order
for troops to quell the fears
of workers at the names
Red Cloud and Little Wolf.
They say the Pawnee
hate the Sioux and so the UP uses them
against their enemy to keep
the railroad safe across this stretch
of contested desert.

       "The train must be
a success," Dodge writes, and so I'm paid
to write the best version

of his vision to tempt
investors, though need for the army
I see everywhere: morale
is fading, enlistment slow.
Even the land is dull here,
coated with salts so all men look
like millers, sage
and truck beds dusted
white, a blankness broken
only by tales some tell
of Cheyenne setting fire
to stage stations and ranches.
Such exploits the workers like
to regale us with, knowing
somewhere between
the boredom, horror, and the glory lies
a story men like me might spin
to lure more settlers
west. How bloodlessly
might we solve the Indian
question if left
to our devices. Senseless
for anyone to fight
when the government can win
with words and time and money.

Our last night as Dodge's
guests, we watched
a train raid staged
for our amusement, the light
of campfire, stars, and moon enlivening
the warriors' features, their yells
and war whoops rising till a chill
flushed through every watcher's
spine. At the sound of our sudden

screams and cries, the warriors
stopped the game and showed themselves
eager only to be paid
for their performance—

                  In the morning,
I watched a band
ride the upper platforms
of the train out into the desert, one
in a gentleman's top hat, another
in breeches of red-
and-blue-fringed leather. They sat—
I telegraphed my readers—and watched
the level plains drag by
beneath them, captivated
by the sights like any citizen,
placid and at ease.

KUNAWOPI AINNI PIKKAHKANTI

有識 / Have Knowledge

Immigration questions for Chinese claiming to be former
US residents, or for Chinese entering the country during the
Chinese Exclusion Act

Have you ridden in a streetcar?
Can you describe the taste of bread?
Where are the joss houses located in the city?
Do Jackson Street and Dupont
run in a circle or a line, what is the fruit
your mother ate before she bore you,
how many letters a year
do you receive from your father?
Of which material is his ancestral hall now built?
How many water buffalo
does your uncle own? Do you love him?
Do you hate her? What kind of bird sang
at your parents' wedding?
What are the birth dates
for each of your cousins; did your brother die
from starvation, work, or murder?
Do you know the price of tea here?
Have you ever touched a stranger's face
as he slept? Did it snow the year
you first wintered in the desert? How much weight
is a bucket and a hammer? Which store
is opposite your grandmother's?
Did you sleep with that man
for money? Did you sleep with that man
for love? Name the color and number
of all your mother's dresses. Now
your village's rivers.
What diseases of the heart

do you carry? What country do you see
when you think of your children?
Does your sister ever write?
In which direction does her front door face?
How many steps did you take
when you finally left her? How far did you walk
before you looked back?

應知 / **Should Know**

A Chinese and English Phrase Book in the Canton Dialect, or
Dialogues on Ordinary and Familiar Subjects, 1888

Lesson XXXIII

You are mistaken.

My store was robbed last night.

The house was set on fire by an incendiary.

He tried to obtain my baggage by false pretenses.

I lost all my clothes and two hundred dollars.

He claimed my mine.

He squatted on my lot.

He took it from me by violence.

I understand every word you say.

The boys annoy me all the time in front of my store.

They break my windows and steal my goods.

Captain, please send a policeman to make them stop.

Please do, for I have to go back to China.

Yesterday was the expiration of one month of my labor.

This boy broke my window.

He pushed me against you.

Please excuse me.

That is the man who cut my head yesterday.

You have no right to arrest me.

悔 / **Regret**

Anthony Trollope, *North America*

This country reels from war. It strains
beneath the weight of an excessive patriotism
which compels the North to crush
all those who dare rebel against
the Stars and Stripes' authority. Nothing
is more tyrannical than strong popular feeling
among a democratic people. Women, too,
a certain class, appear infected by it, who drag
their misshapen, dirty mass of battered
wireworks they call crinolines here
through the station, demanding every
stranger's attention and protection,
while haranguing any man they suspect
of shying from the fight. The touch
of a real woman's dress I find delicate:
but these blows from a harpy's fins
are loathsome. She inserts herself
into the carriage, looks you square in the face,
and you rise from a deference
to your own convictions to give her your seat,
even as men—laborers many, some
infirm or aged—stand to let her pass.
Some matrons even now demand
a private carriage: to guard, they say,
their sensibilities. But I regret I've seen
no delicacy in them, and why should men
expose themselves to cutpurses and ruffians
if they are gentlemen? I wonder, if the train
makes some free to demand protection,
when the tasks now done by men have shifted

to the shoulders of women, will women themselves
complain? What shall they regret
when the spirit of their democracy's reshaped
in the image of their grievance? At night,
in the train, I watch these women rock
in the oil lamps' brassy glow, our carriage gleaming
with teakwood and soft leathers until,
for a moment, all my companions look
companionable, their faces bright, contented,
whole. The train rocks, and the lady
beside me drops her book, and when
I bend to retrieve it, she looks up,
her broad face blushing in the gloam;
for a moment, both of us transported
to some notion of our better selves. Is it sentiment
or struggle that finally cements a nation,
and can strong feeling but only sow
more division when the cause for it subsides,
when we know we do not suffer equally
on account of it? "Union Station," the porter calls,
and a man limps past, his cheek
bisected with a livid scar my female
companion notes with melting sympathy
a moment, before he shrugs his traveling case
close to his side, and once more the lady
turns her face to the window.

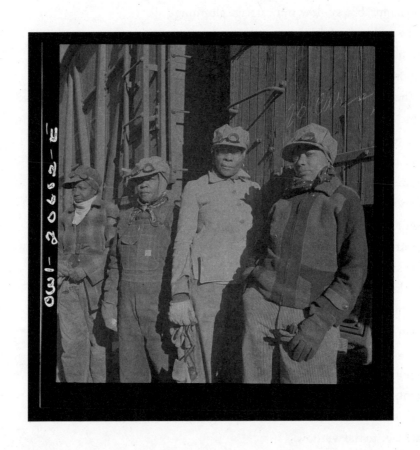

この音は電車の音

No viajamos sobre sobre los rieles.
Los rieles viajan sobre nuestros hombros.

我々は死者を数えられない

Δεν μπορούμε να μετρήσουμε όλους τους νεκρούς

järnvägen åker på oss.

此 / **This**

this is the sound of a train this
is the sound of a train this is
the sound of a train this is the
sound of a train this is the sound
of a train this is the sound of
a train this is the sound of a
train this is the sound of a train
this is the sound of a train this
this is the sound of a train this
is the sound of a train this is
is the sound of a train this is
the sound of a train this is the
the sound of a train this is the
sound of a train this is the sound
of a train this is the sound of
a train this is the sound of a
train this is the sound of a train
train this is the sound of a train

來 / **Journey**

Robert Smithson on Andrew J. Russell's photo *East and West
Shaking Hands at Laying Last Rail*

This excessiveness of men
            spilling, crowding
      to mark their X of time

            and money, I find
                        lamentable—their little moment
                  composed of paper

                  and light: alienated
                              spike, relic
                        in the hands of those willing

            themselves be relics, too. Nothing
                  so linear as human
            ego and desire, while the past

turns and returns, spirals
            like these pelicans journeying
      over the red

            waters off Rozel, streams
                  of purple; yucca rimed
            with pustules of dust.

                  Each one lifts, rises: finds
                              what only some part
                        of the cells remembers, nests

      in the wreck
                  of what we've left, this bulk
            of ruined train, its wheel wells turned

the rust
of flaking blood. Of course
they trekked the human

bodies from the crash
back out. We care
for our own. Or do we care

nothing for our own,
so much material worked from lives
as if to free us all

to forget? Who remembers the names
behind those grasping
fingers in the photo?

Who recalls the dead
the railroad ferried from its crash?
The metals they left

not as memorial to them, but because
it cost less
to leave the evidence

than drag it all back out—

千 / **Thousand**

Wilson's phalarope
Red-necked phalarope
Cormorant
American white pelican
Eared grebe
Great horned owl
California gull
Avocet
Northern shoveler
Bufflehead
Marbled godwit
Canvasback
Common goldeneye
Northern pintail
Mallard
Killdeer
Ring-billed gull
Tundra swan
Western grebe
American coot
Meadowlark
Black-necked stilt
Gadwall
Cinnamon teal
Redhead
Pied-billed grebe
Caspian tern
Forster's tern
Black-crowned night heron
White-faced ibis
Sandhill crane
Snowy egret

Common merganser
Curlew
Great blue heron
Willet
Savannah sparrow
Snowy plover

古 / **Antiquity**

What am I searching for in this dead wreckage,
trestles of bone-spar webbed by orb weavers?
To thumb a slice of ginger bottle, or scratch black
up from burnt opium pipes? To call that body back
in time and hold it, as if object were owner;
and is it honor or indifference to translate material
into person? As if I could wring the song
note by note out of the bird, isolate the dance
from the dancer in this sepia postcard of a Navajo
performing himself for East Coast tourists
who hang, slack-jawed, from train windows.
I want to put that dancer back
into the privacy of history. But he's got his own future.
He's out there now, working on the railroad.

愁 / **Hold Sorrow**

Imagine a farm, a famine, your mother
promised you'll learn tailoring.
Imagine your father pocketing $600.
Now here's the boat, its black
planks wet with fog. Here is the room
holding a bed, no
mirror, your washbasin. You
have one window, wired, to face
the street. He will keep his pants on,
his greasy shirt, his shoes.
Imagine the quarter
pressed after into your palm.
Your street will be named for presidents
you never heard of, the city's lights
like strings of blood in puddles.
Imagine, if you could, you'd carve
your father's name on a knife tip.
At night, only the train cries.
Your door locks from the outside.

1875 page act
↳ forbid chinese women
women in black market
Trafficked chinese women
into west
sold Opium and girls

Chinese prostitution
↳ tricked into it

千 / Thousand

A thousand spades to clear the cuts. A thousand ropes
to haul out redwoods. For the mountains, a thousand arms
to scale the rocks, a thousand hands to lose
in blasts. A thousand corpses frozen in the snow.
A thousand bags of opium, oolong, rice mats. A thousand
and a thousand and a thousand added to each payroll
but not a single name. A thousand shards of pottery
haloing the trestle. Someone's sketched a worker's face
along the flip side of a telegram. He's four dollars
a day, 35 a month. His profile wreathes
like smoke between the numbers.
How many cairns did you say we passed outside Kelton?
Translate these absences to bodies.
Translate these bodies back to men.

古 / **Antiquity**

*An English-Chinese Phrasebook, 1875, and A Chinese and English
Phrase Book in the Canton Dialect, or Dialogues on Ordinary and
Familiar Subjects, 1888*

Lesson XLV

The news now is very old.
He was murdered by a thief.
He was choked to death with a lasso.
He committed suicide.
The English pronunciation is difficult.
But this is Chinese; you must have it translated.
If you find the materials, I will furnish laborers.
Please carry this letter to the post office for me.
Please send this letter.
Shall I continue to wait for an answer?

Oh, Sam, why have you come so late?

恨 / **Bitterness**

Frederick Law Olmsted, *A Journey in the Seaboard Slave States*

"Come, brethren," he sings, "come now,
eoho, eoho, roll away!" And they come to him,
singing, called by this negro—tall, well made—
who's leapt upon the depot barrel.
I watch from my window as one
by one each man pushes his shoulder
to a bale, struggling, straining, singing
his burden up the embankment. A song
I've never heard before, though it seems familiar,
the tune picked up as the music swells
in a confusion of phrases these men
chant back in the manner of sailors
heaving at the windlass. And as they sing,
a lady strolls down my car: her stout,
negro woman trailing; with them
the lady's daughter, and a pretty mulatto.
Heads bowed, the girls sneak confectionary
from the same cone of newspaper. I watch
as the blond one lays her head
upon the colored girl's shoulder, slips
a candy into her mouth, their soft, intimate laughs
not wholly unsurprising to me, as I've seen
such parties as theirs on other trains here
down South, their laughter drowned out
by the tune that thrums around us. Barbarous
and yet, though the words are rough,
not without some plaintive charm.
One by one, the women beside me rock,
the two girls swaying in their seats as if
the song has taken hold of them.

A jumble of petticoats swirls over my feet.
I glance out the window into a negro's face;
he stares up as if to chide me
until I draw back, hastening to turn
away. The heavy thud of bales thunders
into our freight. A slow, scraping groan that seems
to gutter up from the very belly of the train.
The world slides backward. I feel its jerk, the slap
of irons, then the train's greased gait smooths
into a mindless chug. The mulatto smiles,
tracing her reflection in our filmy window—

But that is not her face in the window.
That is my face shadowed there: my darkened
eyes and cheeks, lips almost pretty
in the half-dawn light. Startled, I try
to concentrate upon the world
I'll soon return to: New York, its rush
of crowds; Julia; George; the neat white lines
of children's laundry drying in our garden—
The South slips past, its swaths of green
overspilling every public wall and walk.
The colored girl's eyes meet mine again
and I see a peculiar smile cross her face.
I've seen it here before, that contraction
of the brows and tightening lips—a spying,
secretive, counsel-keeping expression.
Shyly, she offers up a piece of toffee.
But when I slip it on my tongue,
I taste only ink. Sour milk
and newspaper, the sugars
long ago scorched in the stirring.

most extensive s...
These transcontinental roads really comple...
work of Columbus.   He sailed to discover the ...
...and found that his path
...st t...

authorizing
— a name
marking the union
...and also recognizing the sen-
timent of loyalty ... great enter-
prise was ...
this ...

思鄉 / **Miss Home**

Ways to die: blasting accident, derailment,
boiler crack. Crushed between trains crossing
in the night. Electrocution,
bad food, heart attack. You can work
yourself to death, à la John,
à la Henry. Or you can stay at home and die
anyway: fist and noose, club, gun, knife
in the back. Gossip. Sharecropping. Bottle of rum
with gas-soaked rag. What is freedom
but the power to choose
where you won't die? What is a train
but the self once yoked to terror loosed
inside a force that glides
on heat and steam? *You're so far
from Mississippi,* the UP boss said
when we hit Rock Springs. *Don't you miss
your home?*
                    Miss home? I told him.
I'm hoping to miss it entirely.

H: And why did you work for the railroad?

F: I was born in July
and they say that people
born in July like to travel.
But they always come back home.

君 / **You**

Some of the outstanding
citizens in Memphis
was the Pullman
porters. Back
in '43, one outstanding
undertaker in Memphis had
an accident with an old
white guy. The white guy ran
into him in his Cadillac and the cops
started whipping this man, saying, "Boy,
what are you doing
running into this man's car?"
And the white guy said, "It
was my fault," but the cops
just kept beating him. So I said
an outstanding citizen like that
in Memphis, what is there
for me? From what I'd seen
and heard from my grandmother
which raised me—incidentally
she was eight
when the Civil War started—I had
a very good moral background.
She taught me
don't get out there and antagonize
white people. You got
that fear into you, you travel

73

Because
of the war.
It was
either that
or get
drafted,
you know?
And back
in the Second
World War
while all
these husbands
were drafted,
husky, healthy
Black guys
were being
rejected.
A lot of
intelligent, decent
Black guys.
And when they
came home
every white wife
had a Black
boyfriend. Boy,
did they learn
their lesson.
So when
Vietnam come,
they reversed
all that.
It was Vietnam
or the railroad. Boy,
did we learn
that lesson

And then of course, you handle
everybody's linen without
gloves at all, you strip the beds,
you put the dirty linen
in the bin. In the washroom
you handle the dirty
towels by hand, you mop the floor and mop
the smoking room and if
you have any sickness on the train
you clean that up, you use
disinfectant, you debug everything
once a month, you get
to travel, you get some tips.
You always get good
fresh money but somehow
you always leave broke

I worked the bar, selling
liquor and sandwiches and one
day I had trouble with three
white women, they
were pretty high when they
came on. And one asked me
if they could get any liquor, so I
gave them what they wanted
but they started
getting loud and I told them,
You wait until that liquor
dies down if you want more but
she didn't like it. She called me
sunshine: Old Sunshine N——.
Some of them
get loud and nasty. I guess
when you work with them
they are nice sometimes,
then sometimes
they need to let you know
that they are white

Now I'm not telling you
        all of you
feel the same
        way: 90 percent of you
do but there is ten percent
        out there I know
is listening
        to my story and as long
as I respect you, you
        respect me, too,
right? Ten percent.
        The other 90 of you
ain't got nothing
        but leather for me,
boy, I know,
        I'm not lying

And George, would you
        fetch me a drink or get
the paper, George, would you
        have the waiter
come see me, where
        is my connection to
the Parker House, what street
        is South
Central Station on, are taxis
        hard to find, what time
is Chicago, George, please don't forget
        to pick my package up,
George is the name of the man
        who made the Pullman
car, not the name
        I keep inside
my pocket to show them
        I am Albert
my last day on the job

ancestors

Sure, we found our own
        people riding the train
but most time they
        were just stuffed shirts,
you know? They didn't mix
        too well with others, would sit
one place and think
        you should worship 'em.
Which is why I loved
        that man, first time
we ever met. We called him Malcolm
        X, you know
I lost all his letters

Powerful

We should stick together,
they said, because
when you don't have a union,
they treat the porters
any kind of way. And a lot of guys
didn't join until it got to be
a real closed shop. But then we got
stronger, better. And of course
if you got into a hot one
with the conductor, if he
deadhead you
for nothing, short you,
make you pay
75 cents a night
up at Harlem just to sleep,
the Union helps you out. And we
was recognized as real
railroad men. It was beautiful.
That's how we fitted
in. Randolph's Union
let us all be men

You asked what I thought
        about the unions. Well,
this man, he wanted me
        one time to wait on him
upstairs. Of course, he wanted
        to make a date
with me. And I told him,
        which I told a lie, I says,
You bring your wife around,
        I'll bring my husband, but
at that time, I had no husband.
        These things happened
all the time. It wasn't really
        a problem as I never was
a lady's lady, but mister, the unions
        never wanted me

I saw Greta Garbo in my car

I saw soldiers delousing Germans

I saw that black-haired woman down in Washington, she married the guy
who gave up the throne

I was on the dining car when Nixon and Eisenhower was running for president

I shook Miss Ella Fitzgerald's hand

I saw Bing Crosby
Doris Day
Betty Grable
Tom Mix

I remember Marilyn Monroe on my train and oh my gosh

Roy Rogers
Humphrey Bogart
Gloria Swanson

Only Bing Crosby tipped good

So I say to them, I'm a railroad
man, why can't I stay
down at this ten million
dollar YMCA they built
on 44th Street? Well, they said,
We ain't never had men like you
up here. But I
don't give a damn, this
is a YMCA put up
just for railroad people. I'm
as good as an engineer, I'm
as good as a brakeman, I'm
as good as a conductor,
I'm as good as the president even
of the railroad. So I picked up
the fight, and I won that fight
hands down. Oh, I had to get
real radical. And you know
from that night on I broke in there,
Black railroad workers
stay with comfort. They
have a library, pool hall, game
room, they have a cafeteria,
when you open the door, that bed
is spotless. I broke the same thing down
in New Haven. It wasn't tough
because I'd cracked
New York. That's why my wife
tells me, Chico,
if you had stayed on the railroad
they would have killed you

I didn't tell you
        about our youngest
son, he is a handicap
        child. Thirty-one
and he ain't never called me
        daddy yet. But I love
that boy like crazy, boy,
        I'm telling you
I'm crazy about that boy.
        We moved him out
from Brockton in
        September.
You can see the blood
        on this fist, you
can't see blood, but there is blood
        upon this fist.
I had to fight
        the Ku Klux Klan all
over this town. All
        for the privilege
of paying one
        hundred and fifty-
four thousand dollars
        for a house
for that boy to live in

My daughter is a doctor.

My daughter works at the T.

My daughter is the head of the Carney Institute.

My children go to Northeastern now.

My son went to Spellman.

My daughter attended Carnegie Mellon.

My son went to BU .

I sent my daughter to the Ursuline Academy.

I kept after my son, and he woke up late, but he is doing pretty good for himself now.

My son went to Boston Technical.

My son's a mechanic.

I have one son. He is 41.

My oldest girl is a secretary at the John Hancock Building, my other is just a housewife.

My oldest son is in the National Guard.

My son died.

My daughter has two children now.

My child's name is Victory. Named after my father.

Directly the conductor returned to me and said . . . I was in the wrong car . . . To this I replied . . . that I had a seat and intended to keep it. He said to me that he would treat me like a lady, but that I must go into the other car, and I replied, that if he wished to treat me like a lady, he would leave me alone.

> Ida B. Wells, from her legal testimony about being ejected from her seat on the Chesapeake, Ohio and Southwestern Railroad Company train from Memphis to Woodstock

The people in said forward coach where I was were rough, they were smoking, talking and drinking, very rough. It was no fit place for a lady. There were no white ladies.

> G.H. Clowers, African American minister, testimony in defense of Ida B. Wells

空 / **Vainly**

American Etiquette and Rules of Politeness and *The Ladies' Book of Etiquette, and Manual of Politeness,* 1889 and 1860

On the streets, in public
      conveyances, beneath the care

and fret of work, it
      is ever present.

The true secret is you must do
      as other people

do. The polished surface
      throws back

all arrows. Avoid hallooing
      and boisterous talk,

employ a gentleman
      should you require better

service. Give as little
      trouble as possible. Your dress

should be of muslin, your gloves of cotton
      or calfskin leather. Do not pass

through doors or gates or upstairs
      before others. Do not take

the most comfortable seat
      in the room. Arrow in

on acceptable surfaces.
      You are entitled

to certain privileges
       by right of your sex;

for this liberty,
       they will despise you.

The law can touch us
       here and there, now and then,

but in endeavoring to make
       the comfort of others an object

of consideration, never hope
       for any affection

for yourself. Do not look strangers
       in the face. All surfaces

are arrows. In passing,
       turn to the right, attend

your window. Politeness
       forbids any display

of resentment.

對 / **Face**

Andrew J. Russell, official photographer for the Union Pacific

There is one face a man makes
        for the camera, another
for his commanding
        officer. But I don't get close

enough to see.
        I let the gandy
dancers stand as they will
        beside these tracks

our company orders them
        to build: shovel
by shovel mouthed up
        from cold ground. Their shapes,

not their eyes, I am
        to graft
upon collodion. Here
        where the railroad's nerve and flash

tremble over towns
        like packed organs.
Mechanics are the flesh
        I photograph. The men

are just for scale, frames
        to elaborate
a different immensity.
        Not that

[handwritten annotation: — connection between machine and human]

of war, the trenches
         my outfit trolled, scouring
the churned-up fields, sun's
         blank eye staring us down—

Battle remnants I turned
         to stereoscope: each
punched-out hole
         doubled, in its parlor

viewing, to a face.
         What parent, what sweetheart
dared to look?
         The last we took

was of a bloated rebel
         an assistant propped
beside a pile of gravel that,
         in their converging

lines of sight, seemed
         to reach and scratch
my own eyes out.
         The gandy dancers, I'm told,

are former soldiers. Just living.
         The crack of gunpowder
barely stirs them. They laugh
         as they work

in the shelter of this canyon's
         shadow: tender
under its stone
         lip rising like a wave

about to break above them.

望鄉 / **Homeward Facing**

After Hesiod, *Works and Days,* 2.400–500

When summer ceases
    its blister, when autumn rain

cools flesh with downpour
    and thunder, and Mars hangs

high in the sky, wheels
    over stretches of prairie and plain,

gather your returning soldiers: men
    used to hardship and hunger;

make them take up
    ax and blade to harvest timber

whose wood is free of worms.
    Let them hew logs

for cross ties, eight feet
    each; teach them

            — descriptive

to slick lumber with creosote
    and hold the heavy beams

upright, those hundred-pound sleepers.
    And when the spiker comes

with his ash-handled maul, tell them
    look awake: many have split

arms and legs open in the wide
    swings of his windmilling

blows. An experienced man
      needs only three strikes, but mile

after mile nicks metal
      heads, splits handles and wears down

arms and backs and eyes. Young men
      are best at the work

but can't stay the course: they care more
      for riches than reputation

and cannot comprehend the limit
      of their lives. It comes down

to men who know war, so tend all dangers
      with care: men who've bled

know the value of peace, even if they find it
      only in the smoke and cries

of what still sounds to them
      like war. They do not revel

in domestic delights, these warriors
      for whom home is gone

to memory, the nation
      they once knew changed forever

except in the mind, the strain
      of old fears that will not be quieted

by any but familiar labor. And if they scrap
      and fight on the line, know at least

this violence is held back
      from your cities: such is the value

of work that brings men
      back to themselves. This

is how you make men useful
      after war. Now Mars fades and Sirius

rises ascendant. Let your great war
      die in the West. Winter

won't last forever.

Non cavalchiamo sulla ferrov

es el casi hipnotizador sonido

es imposible tratar de contar a todos

os rieles viajan sobre nuestros hombros

臺 / **Terrace**

Of this town once built from redwoods trekked
from the cold Sierras, nothing's left. Just bits
of aqueduct lost by the roundhouse, an outline
ridge of knuckled barrows, glass chips violet
from a century of sun. Fists of clinker,
and on the berm's west side, the ghostly hollows
of Chinese dugouts whose perimeter I trace
according to the wreckage. Shattered
whiskey bottles. Bone dishes ground
into a culvert where I find, thin as a baby's
fingernail, this metal trouser button: its edges
crimped, eyes scrubbed clean of earth so that,
when I peer through its slits, I catch a whiskered glimpse
of jackrabbit, moving so fast not even time can catch him.

未酬 / **Not Fulfill**

Archeological remains from Leland Stanford mansion

hand-painted plaster with floral
pattern   French-
style rose-and-gold wall
paper in the dining
room parlor   sage-
green Venetian glass   German
beer pitcher   Japanese
Kutani teapot and majolica
jardinieres   sofas   bookshelves   brass
rail hooks   hanging
pictures   porcelain
sinks   two bidets   stained
glass window with adorned
fenestrations   lampshades
caster wheels   British
neoclassical vase with scene
of hunters spearing lions
oriental rug
gilded flowerpot

壮志 / **High Ambition**

Archeological remains from Chinese camp near Terrace, Utah

rice bowl shards of four
season pattern   bamboo
green glaze stamped with British
crown   Prosser
buttons   metal
suspender clasps   dozens of flat
cut rectangles of unknown
function   small
vials of liniment   work boots   bitters
carved bone dice
oil-lamp stands and dishes
for pine nuts   rock-
ringed canister with stripe
of excrement   bones
of jackrabbit   porcupine   duck
dish with half
a double happiness on it   lion's
cracked face on the bottom
yawning

埋 / **Bury**

First it was a pocket watch
the archeologists unearthed: its plated chain
strangled inside this grave's

massed roots, black hands clawing
at twelve and two.

                        Trains run
on time as well as coal, the company
owners knew, so that the iron cars
could pass one another
untouched in the dark.

One must invent zones, rules, schedules.
One must assign value

to what threatens the capital, or counts
as a loss—

                        Someone fevers
in his rented room. Someone coughs
and claps a hand to another's back
and a ghost of hours passes

like a shadow straight through you—

Only a matter of time
once the cholera came before they'd point
to us, the company men

who left our bodies where they were felled:
spike handlers, carpenters, Irishmen all

bludgeoned and dumped at Duffy's Cut
beside these tracks

they hired us to build.

壤 / **Soil**

Brigham Young to General Dodge of the Union Pacific, 1869

The locusts' hum, at first, was like a line of flame;
then the air burst into reds, silver-edged
and filled with mouths like snapping scissors.
They ate our wheat, blacked out the skies
until the falling bodies settled like a fog
over Great Salt Lake, the carcasses brined
to a black and growing wall. We thought
the soil here was rich. But who knew how rare
rich was, how terribly fragile, and how
temperamental we'd become
trying to sustain these plots too alkaline
to keep a crop alive. Nothing natural but made
in the beauty of this place. To create a home,
we imported trees and water, we slashed
and burned to excavate a state where nothing
lived, nothing ruled us, and yet in all this nothing
we were subject to the rules nothingness demanded
and allowed, which requires every drop
of blood from our bodies, all that we might plant
and tend and love; that demands all
might still be taken from us and fed to the abyss,
not the faith on which I believe each soul
is nourished. Nothing natural here
but need. Our symbol, as you know, is the hive
of bees, and yet in our strength of will, our number,
perhaps you might picture us now
like the locust, which arrives in waves to feed
without satiety, which visits more regularly
than rain and covers the earth not out of spite,
but because they will survive. Dear General,

all this we have endured, and now you think
we should not remind you of the debt we're owed, we
who lobbied for this railroad, who agreed to unite
this nation with you and bring the riches of the East
west to tame its wilds? Do you wonder
at our anger and our exigency? General,
we worked your grading to Monument Point, in thousands
drilled and blasted, rent the very foundations
of the earth until these hills swarmed with our fresh
encampments. We are patient, but we aren't fools.
If we'd been a collection of mere individuals linked
by money, long ago you'd have seen us crushed
by weather, luck, and the Indian; together in faith,
we have brought this place to heel. We can do more.
Even the locusts, which once again have come
to plague us, make little dent in our labors.
Their dark trails that waver in the heat like iron bars
are merely a mirage, our kerchiefs dipped
in camphor smell not like sweat and earth
but sweet water. They do not stifle, nor blind us
to the promise of the money your company
offered, a promise which has gone, now,
too many months unanswered. We are hungry
for an answer, Sir. We wait for your reply.
Each morning, your railroad tunnel shakes
with the reports of our artillery. You can hear them,
if you listen. The mountains reverberate
from base to summit, ringing back our volleys
with thunderous echoes, as if in anger.

土 / **Earth**

1862 Pacific Railroad Act, Section 2

That the right
    of way through public
lands granted to said

    company for the construction
of railroad and telegraph

        right, power, authority

hereby given to said
        company to take
    adjacent to the line

        road, earth, stone, timber, said

    right of way is granted to the extent
          the United States shall extinguish

all lands falling
    and required for the said

            with the welfare of the said

falling
required for the said
        Indians the said

   grant
     herein made.

Mazacanku akan unkiyankapi šni, iye ca un'akanl inyanke

Dii eé kǫ’ na’ałbąąsii diits’á’

知 / **Know**

Frederick Jackson Turner, lecture to the American Historical
Association, 1893

Come waves of men with capital; come broadcloths,
     silks, leghorns, crapes, all the refinements

the train ushers into each village, and the settler
     revolts, pushes into the interior, flees

what's turned to edifices of brick, orchards, gardens,
     colleges, churches: rolls instead

westward into the frontier's crucible in which
     all former servants of Europe

become American. Without the war cry
     of Cheyenne and Iroquois,

would we be ourselves? Would we have battled,
     consolidated, traded, made self

and liberty our germs of government?
     Would we have stayed

and called home the lands of the upper Yadkin
     had they remained untamed

by farm and corncrib, their timbers not made
     girdled, deadened, fenced?

The West is too much
     for any man. It takes him

from board room and steam engine and loses him
        to birch bark canoe. We see a mountain

and level it; we see a plain
        spread out like a meadow

to overrun: nature the fault and fall line
        we trace to our next

destination, following the arteries
        of our nation's geology: lost shores

of inland seas, shale scarps and carapaces
        carved from eastern Kentucky.

All now replaced by these joins and joints
        of an iron nervous system.

Again and again, we return to the primitive
        line which we alone believe

marks progress; history does not move only forward
        for the American, but back. The settler

will not settle his desires, and so the soul
        of our country stays restless, nervous, intolerant

of administrative experience and education; hews
        to the press of private liberty, which knows

no bounds, gives few benefits, risks
        government laxity and a spoils system.

We are Boone. We are Kit Carson. Hunter, trader, occupant
        of the moment. We are the land

we can't forget once thrived without us. This
     is America, at the end

of a hundred years of life
     under the Constitution.

The train is here. Our frontier is gone.

爾 / **Your**

Sir Richard Francis Burton, *The City of the Saints*

Your republic is a land of misnomers: "America"
not one nation but a continent, your "Indians"
no denizens of any mislocated East.
Even your transcontinental throws its yoke
not across one imagined country
but several: you unable to claim
this territory even of the Mormons, those bloody
hashshashayim, their Brigham Young a Shaykh-el-Jebel
plotting to liberate another newborn Mecca.
Just as in Egypt, I believe this Zion, too,
was plagued by locusts, its Asiatic fields
demolished of maize, the limpid waters so polluted
with carcasses, a thirsty mullah in this desert
would long for beer.
                              Your nation
built a railroad to draw you closer
to the East; now I find the East
already within you. But such a disappointing
version of it! I look in vain for Mormon
out-house harems and find nothing
but farmhouses in which the wives are stored
like any other stock or grain. Polygamy
is conducted with an air of business, the women
married not for sex but because the servants
are more costly here. And yet it's women
over which they would revolt,
these Mormons bedeviled by a government
declaring polygamy and slavery sister
institutions. Congress cannot attack one,
they say, without infringing on the other,

thus "Dixie" do I hear some locals call this place,
their favorite toast, "We can rock
the cradle of Liberty without Uncle Sam
to help us!" Absolute
independence, absolute sovereignty
is their aim, this Deseret exclusive as Tibet
to their defensive faith. Your government fears
a war with China. But the men out here all know
the war will come within.

                    How can you subdue
what you do not truly know, how circumscribe
this globe without a clearer eye for truth?
These Mormons do not even celebrate
your "glorious" 4th, transferring those honors instead
to a later date that recalls their city's survival
from the locusts. On that day, I walked out
of Great Salt Lake to see its cemetery:
the one place both sinner and saint reside
together in peace. There, I found a row
of women tending crosses, heads tucked
as they swept the stones, each one carved
with a gull wheeling in its marble.
Such pretty, powerless things! No hunters
like your famous eagle, though according
to local legend, it was the gulls that came,
and devoured all the locusts.

HELEN'S RESCUE OF TOM.

雄 / **Heroic**

Helen Holmes, *The Hazards of Helen*

Victim? Tie me up
to trestle or bridge,
I bristle, buck: saw

through blunt bindings, swing
& shimmy to ease
myself down burnished

poles. Bold. Cold. Hero-
ic. Lock me inside
your clerk's closet, I'll

pick its double lock,
duck the huckster's ill-
timed shot, tackle rob-

bers in the boxcar.
Intrepid, I ride
astride slender waist

rails, uncouple cars
& mount runaways.
I turn all tails to

heads, begin each film
fired, despised, till I
solve all crises I

alone saw coming.
I get my men. My
fans are manifests

now of different
destinies: the West
is a dead end for

those with frailty in-
built to their machin-
ery. Men here hit

the skids: lost it all
on stocks, cows, cards, slots,
topped out & constrained

by history. But
I'm still specula-
tive, exciting: my

amplitude the end-
less futurity
to which my sex has

always been travel-
ing. That's why strangers
eat me up in the

dark, laugh when I grab
the robber's mitt: the
one snatching at your

heartstrings, my leather
valise. Now I bring
my mouth down to his

wrist to take a bite
that only looks
like a kiss.

心 / Heart

Robert Louis Stevenson, "Across the Plains: Leaves from the
Notebook of an Emigrant Between New York and San Francisco"

"Home, sweet home," the man beside me plays
    upon his cornet, at which all passengers
shout for him to stop. *Sing instead*
    of that good country to which we're traveling,
they cry. *Enough of home!* Enough, too,
    of these cramped cars and killing airs,
these foul malarias that have infected
    half the foreign passengers. We
are the stinking, beating heart of a world
    where pigtailed Chinese pirates rock
beside the broken men of Europe,
    all of it organized and owned
by gentlemen in frock coats with a view to nothing
    more extraordinary than yearly trips to Paris.
Home? My brothers believed their countries
    unfit to house them, and so
have lifted up their heels to find
    another ungrateful country.
Always westward that we run. Hunger
    rushing from the east
while emigrants swarm in equal numbers
    from the opposite quarter: Hungry Europe,
Hungry China. Each one gnawing at the same bone
    until our lips and teeth would meet
and break together. This whole round world
    has been prospected and damned;
there is no El Dorado anywhere.
    Little wonder so many rush
to greet our coming train with warnings now.

Go back! they cry across the plains
of Nebraska, atop the mountains of Wyoming:
　Go back! Go back! And this
is the "good country" to which we're traveling.
　We would emigrate to the moon, it seems,
and never be satisfied. I sit beside a man dreaming of home
　and see again that old, gray, castled sky,
while he conjures up a pagoda and fort of porcelain,
　the train taking us both not just forward then
but back to our eternal musings—
　But back to what? Where are we finally
to be most human except
　on these parallel tracks toward a future
where it is not our use to men of greater means
　that will finally make us brothers?
Hungry Europe, Hungry China.
　Now a passenger lurches to my seat,
a fire of whiskey in his eyes.
　We are in new territory, he declares;
I must come forth to see it. It is a cold,
　moonless night and as we take
the angel seat, I sense, not see,
　the mountains that we pass beside,
their granite walls the heart
　within the heart of night
made more brilliant for its absence of stars.
　Such are the borders of my new country.
I sit with my companion in the echoing black
　and fill my lungs with mountain.

死 / **Dead**

is what they call
a torn-up track
whose living rails I jump
to bed down in the wells
and feel the thud
hit every trestle
steam at dawn
like horses at
the track I trained
before the fillies
foundered sick they fired
the agents vets they fired
the riders me I love
how in a well you thrum
with sound until your bare
lips start to bleed like can
isters of oil I stole inside
the train you'll find a nation
what it wants to eat
and wear and what
it likes to buy a ring
a phone some jeans a Porsche
there is no reason why
to jump a train except to lose
the edges of your self
the time like pacing
Moxie at the track that speed
that almost tears
your hands off at
the wrist she was
the last to go her tendon
bowed and worth less

than insurance no one
rides a racehorse just
for pleasure no one
hops a train if they can take
a plane a car whose engine
speed is gauged by horses kept
alive in memory
for sentiment I guess
there's ghosts
of what we were and are
we cannot bear to leave
out in the desert where
I'm going home just not
right now I said of Moxie
not right now before
the race she hasn't many
left in her you know
she trusts you right
the owner said
then slipped me
two grand and the shots

ry a...

e science of

agitation

unt which t

-ti

 ...cessary ...for an "eight-hour

...ced on railroads; the ...not be

and inde... they di...

不灰 / **Not Ash**

Sui Sin Far, "Leaves from the Mental Portfolio of a Eurasian"

I remember the boy who called me dirty
and the French women who hissed *pauvre*
petite as I passed on the street

and I remember the girl
like me at school who pasted her face
with white paint and blacked her brows
to pass, she said, *as Mexican*—

                         I remember everything
for which I was made to feel

ashamed. Even the fact
my father said I would never make half
the woman my mother was because
of my heart which the doctor now calls
unusually large.

Memory is the weakness
I bear on my own. I come from a race

on my mother's side said to be the most
stolid and insensible, yet feel

so keenly alive
to suffering, it hurts to hear the words
strangers use for Chinese
shopkeepers, or watch

the Chinamen here laugh
when I say I am of their race. I,

who, but for a few phrases, remain
unacquainted with my mother tongue.

                      I have the name
my English father gave me. And I look
like my father; I could be loved

if I lived as if I were like him,
too. But I prefer the name
I have invented for myself.
I want the world

to see my mother in me, regardless
if the Chinese have no souls.

I do not need a soul. It is not my soul

in question here
in these hot glances,
these furious whispers—

                    Why care for love
when I do not know
if I should love others in return?

Love is a white loneliness that swells the heart
and shuts me out from pleasure.
What is there for one like me to do

but wander, a pioneer
traveling between West
and East, myself the link

they threaten to destroy between them.

I do not need a name
on legal papers.

Here is a match. Here is the mirror

in which my pale face burns,
its flickering allegiances.

My soul is everywhere on my person.

I lose nothing of myself
that has not already disappeared.

Sorrowful news indeed has passed to me.
I mourn you: on what day will your wrapped body return?
Unable to shut your eyes, to whom can you tell your story?
Had you known, you never would have made this journey.
A thousand ages now hold the sorrow of a thousand regrets.
Missing home, you face in vain Home-Gazing Terrace,
your ambitions, unfulfilled, buried under earth.
Yet I know death can't turn your great heart to ashes.

Notes Toward an Untranslated Country: An Essay

The Poem: This Chinese poem was carved by an anonymous writer into the walls of the Angel Island Immigration Station, which served as the California detention center for Chinese immigrating to the United States. Detainees were held there for days and weeks, sometimes up to 22 months. Some, facing deportation, committed suicide. This poem, an elegy to one such suicide, is written in regulated verse: eight lines of poetry composed of seven characters each. The closest corollary in English is the sonnet. The Chinese scholar and translator Dr. Fusheng Wu told me that, in regulated verse, two characters form a single unit of meaning, except for the last character, thus the semantic pattern of each line looks like this:

xx/xx/xx/x

In regulated verse, poems are assumed to be autobiographical expression. Here, however, the poet imagines what another has experienced. It is a very unusual elegy, Dr. Wu tells me. This imagination of the other is a violation of its form.

My translation, too, is a series of violations. The Angel Island poem is part of a pair written to and about the same detainee, though I have not included the second poem. The original pair was carved onto the center's walls so that they would face each other: a mirror in the wood of Angel Island, reflecting between them the absence of the suicide. Similarly, the history of Angel Island reflects the history of the transcontinental, since the Chinese Exclusion Act passed in 1882, thirteen years after the first transcontinental was completed. The Chinese, once eagerly recruited to work on the railroad, were no longer of use to the railroad companies. The Chinese Exclusion Act, the first law passed to prevent all members of a specific ethnic or national group from entering the United States, stayed in effect until 1943. The building of the transcontinental is a paired event, just as the Angel Island poem is a paired poem. But though I gesture at both events, I have not included both poems. The reader may sense this exclusion. And yet, what is a translation except a carefully cultivated loss? Into this absence, I lean and angle my mirror.

Sorrowful News: Between April 21 and May 3, 1865, the train carrying Lincoln's coffin traveled through 180 cities and 7 states. Willie, who'd died in 1862 at age 11 from typhoid fever, was disinterred to travel with his father back to Illinois for burial at the family plot. Death is an invitation to return. When I was commissioned to write this poem about the transcontinental by Utah's Spike 150 Committee, my first impulse was elegy. My Gung Gung and Po Po, my maternal grandparents, could trace their lineage to Guangzhou where the Chinese transcontinental workers immigrated from, though my own family has no relationship to the railroad. Po Po was born in Ellensburg, Washington, in 1910, immigrating to Hong Kong when my great-grandfather either fell ill or fled from being murdered by a rival tong leader. She returned to America at age 18, where she met my Gung Gung at an Alaskan cannery. Po Po was American; Gung Gung Chinese. Born in Nam Bin province, Gung Gung immigrated as a paper son to Chicago at age 15. A handsome man and womanizer, he married my homely Po Po because of her English. When he died in 1985 from pancreatic cancer, Po Po held an open casket funeral, though my mother refused to let me see his body. What do we seek from death's display? The day Lincoln's funeral train left on its tour, more than 10,000 people came to watch. The bodies of the Dakota Sioux that Lincoln ordered to be tried and convicted for crimes they likely did not personally commit hung for less than an hour before being dumped in a mass grave. Before morning, their corpses had been excavated by physicians for medical cadavers. Lincoln's funeral car, one of the most elaborately appointed cars built in the 19th century, was purchased by Twin City Rapid Transit Company President Thomas Lowry in 1905. Lowry planned to rehabilitate the car, restoring it to its former glory, but he died suddenly in 1909. In 1911, prairie fires perhaps sparked by passing trains destroyed the car. Its metal couplings and window frames have yet to be discovered, the precious artifacts likely scavenged from the ashes.

Pass: "We do not ride on the railroad," Thoreau writes in *Walden,* "it rides upon us." Thoreau feared the train would destroy small towns as it transported people to cities for commerce and work. And yet he saw the train as lifeline, too, writing of the Fitchburg that it "touches the pond about a hundred rods south of where I dwell. I . . . am, as it were, related to society by this link." This relation both convenience and consequence, connection and strain. "Did you ever think what those sleepers are that underlie the railroad?" he wrote. "Each one is a man, an Irishman, or a Yankee man. The rails are laid on them, and they are covered with sand, and the cars run smoothly over them. They are sound sleepers, I assure you." Driving to Promontory, Utah, with the state historian, I learn that the Irish did compressor work, while the Mexicans and Japanese built trestles and Slavs quarried. Each group hammered down like a spike, yanked up and replaced. From Ralph Waldo Emerson, "The Young American": "[T]he locomotive and the steamboat, like enormous shuttles, shoot every day across the thousand various threads of national descent . . . and bind them fast in one web, an hourly assimilation goes forward and there is no danger that local peculiarities and hostilities should be preserved." Thoreau: "Every path but your own is the path of fate. Keep on your own track, then." As much as Thoreau distrusted the railroad, he was also enchanted by it; he, too, desired to be "a track-repairer somewhere in the orbit of the earth." Tundra swans startle by my window. I drowse as my truck rattles over the sleepers.

Learn: After assuming governorship of California on January 8, 1852, John Bigler, Democrat, enacted policies to prevent Chinese from entering the state. Bigler believed the Chinese never would or should assimilate into American society, and so advocated for the revival of the 1850 Foreign Miners' Tax, with $3 per month levied exclusively for Chinese laborers: about half of their usual $6 income. Not much is known about Norman Asing after his letter to Bigler about these anti-Chinese policies, but Asing, a restaurateur in San Francisco, would likely have been a member of a local tong to guarantee his restaurant's safety in the face of Bigler's policies. Many Chinese men who emigrated to the US and Canada joined tongs: benevolent societies for male workers based on their originating district, family names, or native dialects. Tongs offered protection, but as more tongs rose up in the US, they also turned to organized crime. Tongs are the backbone of Cantonese families. My great-grandfather was a leader in his tong; Gung Gung gambled at the Bing Kong Tong's Wah Mee Club in Seattle, where he was a member. One midnight, when I was twelve, my uncle called to say there'd been gunfire at Wah Mee and no one could find Gung Gung. Actually, there'd been more than gunfire: three Hop Sing Tong members entered Wah Mee and bound, gagged, and shot fourteen people, thirteen to death. It remains the deadliest mass murder in Washington's history. It was also the first time I learned to think of Gung Gung as a man. To me at twelve, a man was foreign, strange, unknown. A man was a dangerous thing. "Foreign," "strange," and "unknown" were words also applied to Chinese throughout the 19th century, though whites rarely considered them men. Their smaller stature, their long gowns and braided queues, along with their work as domestics alongside Irish women, gave them the stereotype of being female themselves. It didn't help that the 1875 Page Act banned Chinese women from our shores out of fear that the Chinese would "breed," turning Chinatowns across the country into bachelor societies. The shock, to railroad men like Leland Stanford or James Harvey Strobridge, was discovering how much physical labor the Chinese could endure. So if they weren't men or women, were they machines? In the body of the present lies the body of the past. Better to erase all trace of the human. Even Lake Tahoe used to be called Lake Bigler, though locals disliked the name. By 1945, "Bigler" had fallen out of use; as a nod to local preference, the California State Legislature finally switched the official name to Tahoe, meaning "big water."

Indeed: "The truth is, they are getting smart," wrote E.B. Crocker of the Chinese transcontinental workers. After stepping down as a California Supreme Court justice, Crocker served as legal counsel for the Central Pacific during its building of the first transcontinental; his comment references the 1867 strike the Chinese railroaders led for more pay. That summer, Chinese workers struggled to complete some of the hardest work on the western half of the Central Pacific line: blasting through the Sierras. A single workday lasted from dawn till dusk, and the Chinese wanted to limit work to 10 hours a day. They also demanded a pay increase from $35 to $40—then $45—a month. The strike infuriated Crocker, who wrote about his struggles procuring Chinese for the Central Pacific as they arrived in San Francisco. "We have proved their value as laborers & everybody is trying Chinese & now we can't get them," Crocker whined in a letter whose language I have cribbed for this poem. Much has been written about the workers' strike by historians. But while others wrote about the Chinese, the Chinese seemed never to write about themselves. Here is the reality of the record: not a single letter, not a sole diary entry written by a Chinese worker has been found. This is not to say there are no records. What is a quote but a fragment of history? What is a newspaper, a land grant act, but one community speaking to the other it wishes to convert? Much can be made of any document, and its language of conformity or deviance, by the reader written into or out of it. Is the phrase book for the foreign traveler a document of the exceptional or commonplace experience? Does the immigrant see himself in the manual's language, or does he become someone who must use that language? The Chinese lost the strike because Crocker cut off their food supplies. Months later, however, the Central Pacific raised their pay. After the transcontinental was completed, Crocker, due to his railroad investments, realized a net worth of a million dollars. He and his family traveled through Europe collecting art, eventually turning their home into a gallery. Interested readers can now visit this museum in Sacramento, open Thursday through Saturday, 10 a.m. to 5 p.m., but closed every Sunday, Monday, Tuesday, and Wednesday.

Sad: Between August 27 and September 15, 1866, President Andrew Johnson conducted his Swing Around the Circle train tour, a series of political rallies universally reviled by the press. Johnson was seeking support for his Presidential Reconstruction policies and certain Democratic candidates in the midterm elections. Johnson's own lenient Reconstruction policies allowed Southern states to revert to their prewar social system, which led to the proliferation of Jim Crow laws across the South. Johnson's temper, his poor speaking skills, along with the fact he'd been drunk at his own inauguration, led reporters to label him a "vulgar, drunken demagogue who was disgracing the presidency." Johnson's speeches were politically ineffective but incendiary nonetheless. In Indianapolis, gunfire broke out between Johnson supporters and opponents, resulting in one man's death. In Johnstown, Pennsylvania, a temporary platform built for the rally broke, sending hundreds into a drained canal and killing thirteen people. Johnson's speaking tour became one of the centerpiece arguments for his impeachment in 1868; other articles focused on his removal without congressional approval of Edwin Stanton, the secretary of war whom Johnson personally disliked. Johnson was impeached once, for abuse of power and obstruction of Congress; President Donald J. Trump was impeached twice, the first for abuse of power and obstruction of Congress, the second for inciting the insurrection that took place after his rally on January 6, 2021. He was acquitted by the Senate both times. When a man stands behind a platform calling another man a virus, what is the reach of this language? From 1882 to 1968, at least 4,743 lynchings occurred in the United States; 72.6% of the murdered were Black. The FBI reported that hate crimes in the US rose in 2020 to the highest level in more than a decade. By August 2021, the group Stop AAPI Hate had received 9,081 reports of racially motivated attacks since the COVID-19 pandemic began. More than 63% of these reports were filed by women; a little more than 60% of these hate crimes occurred on public streets and in businesses. On March 16, 2021, six Asian American female workers in Atlanta-area massage parlors were shot and killed by a young white man claiming he had a sex addiction. *Go the fuck home,* someone spray paints on my cousin's garage. *It's OK to be white,* reads the poster someone tapes up outside my office building. Echoes or return? Spiral or progress? The English poem reflects the Chinese, but it is not the same poem. The railroad is not the example but a prism of us. Lay another sleeper down in that sentence. The *us* in the sentence is the slap.

Lament: The loss of the sequoias is one part of the transcontinental's environmental impact. The rise of coal is another. The near extinction of the American bison, facilitated by better preservation techniques for hides, which allowed factories to turn the skins into conveyor belts. Prairie fires sparked by passing trains. Echo and Weber Canyon and the great Sierras carved up with cuts and tunnels. Wheat and livestock agriculture exploding by 340%. State economies changed from a barter to a cash system. Silver ore, lead, and coal mined and shipped out of the West. Also, the invention of the Sierra Club, the rise of national parks. If you drive toward Sacramento across the Lucin Cutoff that bisects the Great Salt Lake, you'll see the water on the south arm is green, on the north arm, violet. The Lucin Cutoff, built first by the Southern Pacific, which acquired Central Pacific operations and is now owned by the Union Pacific, is the causeway intended to trim the transcontinental's distance and bypass Promontory Summit. Water between the lake's divided sides does not travel. The green comes from salt-loving plants called halophytes; the violet from the bleed-off of carotenoids, pink pigments in brine-shrimp and brine fly larvae. If you take the I-80 route out from the Lucin Cutoff, you'll wend through the Pilot Range and Great Salt Lake Desert, owned and protected by both the Union Pacific and US military. After 9/11, Hill Air Force Base built a fake village on the flats and bombed it for practice. To our military, Utah resembles Afghanistan. Ralph Waldo Emerson: "The railroad is but one arrow in our quiver . . . The land is the appointed remedy for whatever is false and fantastic in our culture." When I look out my truck window, I can just make out an old Morton Salt billboard. Wood loading platform, roadway memorial, "Russell" spelled out on the salt flat in stones. The bombs, the state historian warns me, didn't all go off when they were dropped. Never leave the safety of the road. Truck tire rusting in the salts. When it rains, it pours.

What Day: Canadian filmmaker Richard Fung opens *Dirty Laundry: A History of Heroes* with a scene of a train steward reading a magazine article headlined "Canada's Railway: A Symbol Under Threat." A few shots later, this same steward is locked in an embrace with a journalist named Roger Kwong, who's traveling across the Canadian Rockies to research his family's history with the train. The two men's encounter is interspersed with historical footage of the train hurtling through tunnels, the train moving both backward and forward at once, the men's sex overlaid on the technology Kwong's family helped build. Is the train, in its disruption of time, where we lose or find ourselves? My father recalls traveling back to Seattle from his East Coast college on the transcontinental, during which time he shared a car with a young child and her mother. One night, he woke to find the child crying, the mother gone. When he went in search of her, he found the woman in a darkened corridor, skirt hiked up, legs wrapped around another passenger. "It changed my picture of women forever," my father said, disgusted. I laughed. Move your hands into the dugout dirt: you can feel the nestle of bodies, the soft silt of skin and hair. Translation of a Man into Labor. Translation of a Man into Need. And what is that translation? Humiliation or rage or desire? We never stop building the railroad.

Wrap: Between 1820 and 1860, the Irish composed one-third of all immigrants to the United States and were the primary early builders of the Central Pacific Railroad. Cholera, which appeared in the US in 1832, was little understood in terms of causes and transmission. Due to prejudice and the high number of Irish immigrants, however, Americans believed the Irish caused cholera, which broke out in separate epidemics in 1832, 1848, 1866, and the 1870s. The bulk of letters I found by Irish writers mention cholera; many of them lament their move to the States. The Irish, like the Chinese, worked as domestics as well as railroaders; the Irish, like the Chinese, were almost universally despised. Help Wanted ads in local papers had codes to indicate preference for English or Scottish maids: *Clean Protestant Girl Wanted.* The Irish, like the Chinese, left their nations under foreign occupation, riven by war, depleted by famine. They, too, suffered from US immigration policy. Between the 1840s and 1870s, as many as 50,000 Irish were expelled from Massachusetts under its policy of deporting foreign paupers; thus, the Irish were the first targets of our nation's deportation laws. There are, however, no Irish Exclusion Acts. And though both the Irish and Chinese were paid poorly by the Central Pacific, the Irish made $5 more a month, plus lodging. Unlike the Chinese, the Irish believed they would stay in America, thus never return home. Unlike the Chinese, they did not create elaborate death rituals to ensure their bodies would get sent back, their death not imagined as a final resistance to this nation they saw first as a place to make money. The Irish, like the Chinese, understood some part of their lives to be transactional in ways that, perhaps—in our desire to see ourselves first as free and equal to others—we overlook. In the end, the Irish, like the Chinese, found themselves with one foot on the rail, one foot in memory. And at all times, they had their bodies to contend with.

Body: As part of their death rituals, Chinese workers would pay a *huiguan,* a district association, to bury their bodies, then have a bone collector exhume them months later to scrape away the flesh and break the bones up to fit into earthen jars or wood boxes. These boxes would then be shipped to Hong Kong to the Tung Wah Hospital, which would distribute the remains to the workers' families. The man may die on foreign shores, but he always returns home. Bones were shipped from San Francisco to Hong Kong as early as 1855. No one knows how many Chinese workers died building the railroad as the Central Pacific kept no casualty records, so no one knows how many coffin boxes linked to the railroad were shipped to China. And not all men's bones were collected once returned. I am sent a video by a mixed-race artist named Summer Mei Ling Lee who has documented the hundreds of boxes abandoned in Tung Wah's mortuary. In her video, Lee paints an art gallery with scenes from Guangzhou in ash ink made from burnt incense. I am startled by the detail of her scenes. Lee depicts houses, roads, villages. Many images include seabirds, which reminds me of something Po Po once said about the cormorant, the bird whose neck fishermen fitted with a tight ring so the bird could catch fish but never swallow them, as it could never swallow the souls of the dead it hunted on the seas. "Why would birds hunt souls?" I asked Po Po as a child. "Because," she said, "some people never find themselves anywhere, in life or death." In her video, Lee stands before her installation in the tiny San Francisco Chinatown gallery. *She looks white,* the gallerist says to the audience in Chinese. *But she is one of us.* The artist flinches as if slapped. The camera catches the flinch. I am at home, watching the flinch on my screen.

Return: The Chinese believe the living possess two souls: *hun,* the light, male, active spirit that gives us our spark of life; and *po,* the dark, female, passive spirit which animates our flesh. In death, the male spirit ascends to heaven; the female part remains on earth. *Falling leaves return to roots:* a Cantonese saying about the return of the dead to their homeland. But not everyone cares which leaves fall. Women, children, those who died a violent death were buried without ceremony, remaining where they died. I think of the Angel Island suicide. I think of Gung Gung and our family's July firecrackers, the sparklers he nudged into my fists. It was a point of pride for him that all three of his sons joined the US military, though one, Kingsley, nearly died. Once I asked Po Po what she considered the best day of her life and she told me, "The day your uncle King returned home from Vietnam." If my uncle had died in that war, his body would have been closer to his parents' ancestral homeland, but not his own. It is possible he might never have been recovered. We treat the elegy as a pathological mode, the mourner incapable of resolving loss. But what if the point of grief is not its resolution but the extension of memory, the insistence that the listener, too, carry our history into the future? Po Po bowed her head as she wept in front of me, her body not making a single sound. "What about the women?" I ask Lee on the phone when I interview her about her installation. "I drew a face," she says, "in one window. You can just see her if you look." The video pans by the houses. On the white screen, a blur of ash.

Not: Dennis Kearney was an Irish immigrant who in 1877, along with J.G. Day and H.L. Knight, founded the Workingmen's Party of California, an American labor organization formed in response to high unemployment caused by the 1873–78 national depression. Members of the Workingmen's Party of the United States participated in the Great Railroad Strike of 1877, which began in West Virginia and spread to New York, Pennsylvania, Maryland, Missouri, and Illinois, leading to the burning of railroad stockyards and buildings, and the deaths of at least 100 people. After the California party won a significant number of seats in the California State Senate and State Assembly, it rewrote the state constitution to deny Chinese citizens voting rights. It also wrote into the constitution the California Railroad Commission, which oversaw the activities of the Central and Pacific Railroad companies. The party's anti-Chinese sentiment helped fuel support for the 1882 Chinese Exclusion Act. Nearly 150 years later, ostensibly concerned that Chinese nationals at US universities were stealing state or technological information, the Trump administration canceled the visas of more than a thousand Chinese students and researchers in the United States who had direct ties to universities affiliated with the People's Liberation Army. In fall 2020, Secretary of State Mike Pompeo said he wanted China's government-funded Confucius Institutes, which have branches on university campuses across America, shut down. The US State Department also announced that the entry of senior Chinese diplomats to US campuses would require State Department approval. Lectures were canceled, fellowships revoked. Universities, unsurprisingly, balked. My own institution, the University of Utah, includes a Confucius Institute which Dr. Fusheng Wu directs. It is directly responsible for funding this project.

Able: The poems "Able" and "Should Know" take their language directly from *A Chinese and English Phrase Book in the Canton Dialect, or Dialogues on Ordinary and Familiar Subjects*, 1888. Did Gung Gung use these phrase books when he arrived in America? "A shame he never learned English," my white uncle said after Gung Gung died. "He seemed so intelligent." When Gung Gung died, he left behind a photo album filled with snapshots of girls he once knew and perhaps dated. In between these photos he added poems in Chinese, jokes in English, doodles drawn in white crayon. Along one side of an opera singer's snapshot is the cartoon of a man's boot kicking a Chinese man in the ass. "Get out, you bum!" Gung Gung scrawled along the side. I spent almost every weekend of my childhood trailing Gung Gung in his garden or sitting in his makeshift woodshop watching as he built a balsa stable for my model horses. I have no recollection what language we spoke. Now I try to recall a single thing he said to me. Only the guttural drag of his voice, the low sound of his laugh. I read his photo album now instead. Gung Gung was a wonderful artist.

Close Eye: Between 1854 and 1929, over 250,000 children were sent by train from New York City orphanages to the West to be adopted. Charles Loring Brace of the Children's Aid Society implemented the first orphan train, as it came to be known. The New York Foundling Society and the New York Juvenile Asylum (later the Children's Village) also arranged orphan trains. The plan was to decrease the number of abandoned or poor children on the East Coast. According to a 1913 Iowa *Anchor* article, "Homes are desired . . . in both town and country but they must be good homes where influences are of the best and under no circumstances will a child be placed with people who wish chore boys or kitchen drudges." Children as young as infants and as old as seventeen were accompanied by nurses and Sisters of Charity to towns across the Midwest and Texas, distributed to any family who made application. Unlike contemporary adoption practices, many of the parents neither applied to nor were approved by a social services agency; some children were adopted by passersby, or those lured to the station by circular letters. Many children were immigrants or children of immigrants, specifically German, Irish, and Italian. Almost none were African American as the Children's Aid feared they would be worked as slaves. The orphan train later implemented regulations, including home visits, to ensure families did not abuse their wards. That said, here is one 1890 newspaper account of the open-market adoption process in Hebron, Nebraska, that leaves me cold: "The greatest contest was for possession of a sweet-faced modest girl of fourteen. There were as many as a dozen wanted her." My own Gung Gung was adopted, twice. The first by my great-grandfather, James, so that his wife would have company after he left for America. The second by my great-uncle, Howard, who lived in Chicago and legally claimed Gung Gung as his son. Once Gung Gung arrived in Chicago, Howard put him to work painting vases for his shop: pagodas and opera singers copied from magazines, misty hillsides, scraps of poems. Gung Gung painted them on soy sauce bottles that Howard then sold as antiques. Most Chinese American families have stories like this; it wasn't till college that I understood many of my uncles weren't related to me by blood but paper. Are all families as arbitrary, as fragile? The orphan train only ended after the emergence of organized foster care. Perhaps you wonder what happened to that girl in Hebron. Perhaps, like me, you are afraid to find out.

To: What's missing in this list of transcontinental stops are the towns, section stations, and freight sidings through Promontory Summit killed off by the Lucin Cutoff after the steel tracks were pulled up to make munitions for World War II. The last scheduled passenger train through Promontory station was Sunday, September 18, 1904. Railroaders call the old transcontinental line "the dead." Here is the list of the dead: Corinne Junction, Balfour, Conner, Blue Creek, Lampo, Surbon, Promontory Summit, Rozel, Metataurus, Centre, Lake, Kosmo, Monument 10-Mile (Seco), Nella, Kelton, Elinor, Kelton, Zias, Peplin, Ombey, Romola, Matlin, Gravel Pit, Red Dome, Terrace, Old Terrace, Watercress, Walden, Bovine, Medea, Old Lucin, Umbria Junction. If you have a good truck and there is no snow, you can visit the dead. *No trespassing* read signs on both sides of this road.

Who: This is a list of the western tribal lands between Ogden and Sacramento that the transcontinental crosses. I'd first imagined this as a poem composed of documents written by members of these nations, but of course each experienced the railroad's construction differently. Lakotas, who hunted across expansive territories, had their food supplies significantly reduced by the railroad. Cheyennes, whose economy was shaped around intertribal trade which the transcontinental disrupted, cultivated treaty-based annuity economies and turned to raiding. Some Pawnees became US military employees. Shoshones, driven from their territories by the Mormons, were awarded free riding privileges for their acquiescence to the railroad—only atop train roofs. In the absence of specific voices, then, I present this general document that suggests the specific. Which is to say, I recognize that in writing about the railroad, every inclusion means exclusion. I understand that for some readers the poem that evokes the past is meaningful only if it moves beyond the informative to the affective detail. The poem asks you to feel where history asks you to remember. But perhaps the affective detail resides in silence placed alongside other silences. History, then, may be best understood as a question of relation. According to report, Chinese railroaders, like their white counterparts, were suspicious of the native people they encountered. The early Chinese imagination of America thus encompasses the indigenous even as it also negates it, just as the Miwoks' territory included Angel Island, though not its immigration station. How, exactly, do I both extricate and combine these narratives to write movingly about them? Or should you *feel* anything at all? Is it poetry or history that finally becomes the archive's most controversial translation? The slap in the document is the poem.

Tell: Telegraph and transcontinental tracked each other, just as later the national highways tracked the transcontinental. One infrastructure builds the next. In 1868, telegraph wire was used by the Sioux to tie together a blockade of wood pilings to derail a train. Telegraph wires were also destroyed in Julesburg and across the Platte Valley by warriors assembled from the Sioux, Northern Cheyenne, and Arapaho tribes in retribution for the Sand Creek massacre in Colorado Territory, in which Colonel John Chivington ordered his regiment to murder 230 Cheyennes and Arapahos, mostly women and children, saying, "Kill and scalp all, big and little; nits make lice." Chivington's soldiers mutilated the corpses, some claiming genitals as prizes. After the northern Plains Indian retribution for Sand Creek at Julesburg, General Grenville Dodge, who later became chief engineer of the UP, led a campaign against the Plains Indian tribes, sending General Patrick Edward Connor out to chase after the dispersed war parties. Connor attacked a peaceful settlement of Arapahos on Tongue River, killing around 200 men, women, and children. Largely, the northern Plains Indians stayed clear of the railroad, though the railroad and the US military did not stay clear of them. In 1866, Captain William J. Fetterman, stationed near the Bozeman Trail, claimed he could "ride through the whole Sioux nation" with just 80 soldiers. Despite orders to avoid confrontation, Fetterman and his soldiers were lured by a party of warriors led by Crazy Horse into a waiting group of Cheyennes, Lakotas (Oglala, Brulé, and Miniconjou), and Arapahos. No US soldier survived. Intertribal conflict between the Sioux and Pawnee meant that Dodge and the Union Pacific would later hire Pawnee scouts to protect the railroad from the Sioux who, though they rarely harassed the line, were reported by telegraph to be menacing the transcontinental's progress. Under the direction of Major Frank North, a battalion of 200 uniformed Pawnee scouts patrolled the line to act as deterrents. "I have never seen more obedient or better behaved troops," raved one of North's superiors. One infrastructure enables another. For the 1876 Centennial Exposition in Philadelphia, over 300 American Indians from 53 nations were transported by train, along with a Corliss steam engine, a 15-foot walrus, sharks, and a polar bear. The highlight of the exhibition, however, was Alexander Graham Bell's newest invention: the telephone.

Have Knowledge: According to the many documents gathered by my uncle King, Gung Gung's last name is either Jian, Jon, Con, Gonn, Kwan, Khan, Ghan, Quan—all variant renderings of a character that only resemble its pronunciation. We called him Gung Gung, ah gung. His American first name was George. His Chinese first name was Jan. Born in Guangzhou Province in 1906, he celebrated his birthday each September 22, though later he said he was born in August. No papers exist to confirm or deny this. His own father's name is Chao Ze, Sui Jok, Sui Ja, or James. James was born sometime in the mid-19th century. He is, as I wrote before, not Gung Gung's real father. At Angel Island, details such as these became crucial, as detainees were interrogated with questions only authentic applicants should know. To ensure they were telling the truth, witnesses from across the country might be called in, usually people claiming to be family members who would then corroborate the detainee's lies. Do we invent or do we inherit a self? Gung Gung loved fish and playing checkers, and his garden. He collected stamps and he built cabinets and he drove a cab. He was the only member of his family to welcome my white father after his proposal to my mother, inviting him and my paternal grandmother, Irene, to a secret meeting one afternoon when Po Po was out. Po Po returned home early, found my father and Irene strategizing with Gung Gung on her couch and, out of humiliation and pride, wordlessly served them coffee. Angel Island operated from January 21, 1910 to November 5, 1940. After it closed, the US Army turned it into a processing center for those it deemed prisoners of war. Not an invention but a poem. Not a poem but a man. How much of this man will I uncover? X marks the spot.

Should Know: Here are the places in the West where Chinese residents were lynched, massacred, murdered, or attacked on account of their race during the 19th century:

Bellingham
Seattle
Issaquah
Newcastle
Tacoma
Olympia
Tekoa
Portland
Oregon City
Albina
La Grande
Hells Canyon
China Gulch
Denver
Bonners Ferry
Pierce
Oro Grande
Eureka
Redding
Chico
Truckee
San Francisco
San Jose
Fresno
Selma
Pasadena
Los Angeles
Butte
Reno
Tonopah
Rock Springs
Vancouver
Farmington
Port Townsend
Monterey
Hamer

Little Butte Creek
San Pablo
Stockton
Juneau
Modesto

Regret: Anthony Trollope's *North America* was published in 1862, nearly thirty years after his mother Fanny's best-selling *Domestic Manners of the Americans* appeared in England. Fanny (Frances) Milton Trollope had moved to America in 1827 to join the abolitionist Nashoba Community with three of her children, leaving Anthony behind in England with his father, Thomas, a failed lawyer with larger social ambitions than his means would allow. Miserable and bullied at school, Anthony Trollope seems to have been ashamed by the social pretensions of his parents. Failure dogged the Trollope family. Fanny and Thomas's marriage foundered, and the Nashoba Community collapsed after rumors began about the residents' practice of free love and interracial marriage. Fanny appears not to have engaged in interracial relationships at Nashoba, though she did become intimate with the French artist Auguste Hervieu, moving with him to Cincinnati to open a bazaar, which failed. Fanny returned to England in 1831, where she became a hit with the publication of *Domestic Manners,* whose negative portrayals of Americans—which delighted the English—were not well received by Americans. Anthony Trollope's *North America* was a critical revision of his mother's travelogue, perhaps also a dig at the mother who abandoned him as a child. Hers, he says in his introduction, was "essentially a woman's book." During her life, Fanny published six travelogues, thirty-five novels, and countless articles and poems. During his, Anthony wrote forty-seven novels, one memoir, four travelogues, and six collections of short stories. Both Trollopes were popular, both wrote for money, both were reviled by critics for the same. Trollope's best novels, in fact, are portraits of jealousy and money: *He Knew He Was Right,* a study of a man's sexual jealousy over his wife, and *The Eustace Diamonds,* a mystery about the corrupting influence of money on desire. Throughout his later novels, however, Anthony returned to the cultural problem that, for him, America symbolized, depicting the differences between British and Americans as finally a familial dispute. Their closeness, he argued, throws small differences into high relief. Perhaps our nations are more intimate with each other than they'd like.

This: At the 2018 conference for the Chinese Railroad Workers Descendants Association, I take audio recordings of conferees saying one of three sentences: "This is the sound of a train"; "We do not ride on the railroad, it rides upon us"; and "We cannot count all the dead." These lines are for a video project I am completing. Those who speak Cantonese, I record saying the lines in their mother tongue. I cannot, however, get anyone to approximate the quote from Thoreau. "There is no way to say this in Chinese," one man says, shaking his head. Po Po and Gung Gung, fluent in Cantonese, are not alive; I cannot ask my mother for a translation. My mother does not fully comprehend Cantonese and, I understand, is embarrassed about this, among other things. One afternoon, over lunch, she leans across the table with its pot of tea steaming between us and says she's sorry she moved me as a child from the Asian-dominated Beacon Hill to the whiter enclave of Ravenna. "We did it for the schools," she says. "But now you are more comfortable among white people than us." The *us* in this sentence is the slap. There is a little too much emphasis my mother puts on "us." The final, forceful way she places her teacup by the bowl. Of course, I am not finally responsible for that decision or its attending comforts. I recall an afternoon in high school sitting on Po Po's couch with my mother, Po Po's friends smiling and staring at me. *She's so pretty and white,* someone murmurs to Po Po, and my mother grinds her hand into my knee.

Journey: Robert Smithson (1938–1973), one of the founders of the influential Land Art movement, was best known for his artwork *Spiral Jetty*, built on the northeastern shore of the Great Salt Lake near Rozel Point. Composed of mud, salt crystals, and basalt rock, the *Jetty* forms a 1,500-foot long and 15-foot wide counterclockwise spiral curling from the lake's shore. No one knows exactly why Smithson chose Great Salt Lake to build the *Spiral Jetty*, though the most prevalent theories have to do with the transcontinental. Smithson was taken by the violet color of the lake caused by the Lucin Cutoff, which isolates the saline-heavy waters from freshwater sources. But Smithson may also have been attracted to Rozel Point's proximity to the Golden Spike National Historic Site where the Central Pacific and Union Pacific lines met: its X of connection forever stamped on the map. An X whose shadow lingers, too, in the visual composition of Andrew J. Russell's iconic "Champagne Photo." The Golden Spike suggests linear completion; the *Spiral Jetty*, unfurling and return. A rejection of progress, a revision of history. It is the act of cycling back through time. Driving the causeway now, the Lucin Cutoff takes you past both Rozel and the remains of the Bagley train wreck, in which a mail train plowed into the back end of a slowing passenger train one December morning in 1944. Fifty people were killed, mostly military personnel, 80 others injured. About the meaning of his work, Smithson said that he wanted to document "the earth's history." Entropy and decay obsessed him; Smithson believed all systems devolve over time to equilibrium. One art critic friend admits the *Jetty* is less interesting as disordered history, however, than in how it disrupts the art market; the Dia Foundation protects it, but no one can claim to really *own* it. From my truck, the horizon's salinated haze blurs sky and water: a flock of birds swims past like fish. The Bagley train wreck has never been removed from the causeway because it was too expensive to tow out. You can drive to it now, walk between the ruined cars. The rust resembles rock, the wheels eroded to sand. Over decades, the train wreck has softened into landscape, the *Jetty* crystallized into Art.

Thousand: This poem is a partial list of the 250 species and ten million birds that migrate each year to the Great Salt Lake's Bear River Migratory Bird Refuge and over the dead transcontinental. This list is inspired by Summer Mei Ling Lee's avian paintings, composed to reflect the Chinese belief that birds carry the soul from one land to the next. Bear River is now suffering the effects of a 40-year drought in the West, with the result that thousands of birds have died off. Neither the transcontinental nor the refuge can offer safe passage here. The dead transcontinental weaves just beyond Bear River, its proximity to the refuge less choice than historical accident. And yet of all the sections of the railroad, this accident feels to me the most deliberate, the most ironic, and perhaps because of this, for me the most personal.

Antiquity: While the Diné did not build the transcontinental, they are now the largest national group working to maintain it and the lines radiating out from it across the West. How many of them have worked on the railroad and for how long is not known. *Metal Road,* Sarah Del Seronde's documentary of the Union Pacific's 9001 Heavy Steel Gang and its Navajo workers, opens with this 1868 quote from *San Francisco Chronicle* correspondent W.H. Rhodes: "At present time, there are about 10,000 Chinamen, 1,000 white men, and any number of Indians employed on the road." *All that wheels and grease do a number on a line,* one of the Diné workers tells Del Seronde, looking away from her camera. The camera follows his gaze. Long track of sun beating down the line. *Rail's just another piece of equipment.* And the wood degrades, the irons heat up in the sun. *Valentino, Virgil, Junior and me, we're working for the 9001. Worked here 20 years. But not straight. And without the straight months, you never get benefits.* Benefits, of course, matter most. When Del Seronde asks a white supervisor why the 9001 hires Diné, he tells her, *The kind of work that we do fits the kind of life Navajos lead. They are a very rough, tough people. Extremes do not affect them the way they affect other people.* Metal expands, pops the bolts. Another Diné worker limps past with a T-shirt reading *Indians make the best cowboys.* And the track loosens, starts to pull away from itself. *Got bit by a brown recluse,* he tells Del Seronde. *Lost my leg.* Union Pacific logo sewn onto his pants. *Oh, you beautiful, you perfect railroad men!* sings the supervisor to the workers each dawn. The Diné worker had to pay for his own leg treatments. *You know,* he tells the camera, *you never quit building the railroad.*

Hold Sorrow: Chinese prostitution in the US is a legacy of the tongs who trafficked Chinese girls into the States—in some cases under the false impression they would be given to an eligible man in marriage, more often as kidnapping victims. Many believed they'd entered into an indentured servant system that contractually required they serve as prostitutes for a specific period of time, but because Chinese women could not read, they didn't understand the contracts. Between 1852 and 1873, the Hip Yee Tong alone brought in around 6,000 women to San Francisco, about 87% of the total number of Chinese women that arrived on the West Coast, netting an estimated $200,000 from their sales. After the 1875 Page Act, which specifically targeted Chinese women entering the country, trafficking only became more lucrative. A woman bought for $50 in Canton could now be sold for $1,000 in San Francisco; in the 1890s it was reported that a single woman went for $3,000. When I interview Willy Chun, the 93-year-old leader of the Bing Kong Tong in Salt Lake, none of this is discussed. Bing Kong Tong is a transcontinental holdover in Utah, the state's only warrior tong sent east in the 19th century by its San Francisco founders to secure the Utah Territory. Like Hip Yee, Bing Kong Tong trafficked opium and Chinese girls through the West, ensuring that Chinese money went back into Chinese pockets. Bing Kong either instigated, or finished, one of the most violent tong wars in American history. But all that is in the past. Now the tong gives money for scholarships and offers prayers for the dead transcontinental workers, Willy tells me. Bing Kong is dying out because the Chinese coming to the country are not working men from the south like Gung Gung, a member of Bing Kong's Seattle chapter. They are Mandarin speakers with wealthy families and good educations. At the tong's meeting hall on State Street, Willy pulls out a battered briefcase to show me the documents the tong has collected from the past century. The papers are a messy stack, photos and member enrollments and charter documents tossed together. In one corner sit the tong's last members, restaurant cooks and construction workers. They smoke and play mah-jongg on the new mechanized table Willy has bought them. They look embarrassed when I approach. *Why are you a writing a poem about us?* one asks in Cantonese. Before I tell him the truth, my translator interrupts. *Because someone wants her to praise us,* he answers.

Thousand: If you have stood in the sleet. If you have stood in the wind. If you have put your hand to the ground and felt the cold burning up from stone or walked the quarter-mile grade dug out of earth, shovel by shovel. If you have seen bridges hammered into sides of granite or stood at Dove Cut to find every foot there planed, tamped, packed. Every iron bit hammered into place, every mountain groined by blasts of nitroglycerin. To know that eyes were lost here, as well as hands and limbs and skin and face. Then you come close to something like awe. The evidence moves you to pity, to dread, almost to mirth. A human task done for the inhuman. And if you have looked, you cannot help but feel it all press up and through you, this work designed to destroy the body, destroy the mind, to make you senseless as whatever piece of steel you grip in your hand. A crush of time. The whole earth bisected by it. And you, free over it all, never free from it all, walk the line.

Antiquity: And is it work or bodies I wish to resurrect, or just a better version of my nation?

Bitterness: Frederick Law Olmsted (1822–1903) was a clerk, sailor, landscape architect, farmer, social critic, journalist, and public administrator, all without the benefit of a college education. He is best known for designing Central Park, the Niagara Reservation in Niagara Falls, and the landscape around the United States Capitol building. Olmsted's journalistic interest in the slave economy led to a commission by the *New York Daily Times* to travel across the American South and Texas between 1852 and 1857. One of Olmsted's memoirs from this time, *A Journey in the Seaboard Slave States,* contains his observations of enslaved railroaders singing while loading freight in South Carolina. It is the first journalistic recording of Black railroaders' songs. Slaves built most of the antebellum South's 8,764-mile network, while also working as firemen, brakemen, and switchmen. The southern railroads also rented slaves out from individual owners to load freight cars; by 1860, the southern railroads used the labor of nearly 15,000 slaves. According to the scholar Theodore Kornweibel, Jr., the largest single concentration of enslaved railroaders may have been on the North Carolina Railroad which, in 1852, worked 1,493 men and 425 boys; no single plantation held as many enslaved people. The slave system on the southern railroads created a racial employment pattern across the states that would last decades: the most dangerous or physically demanding jobs, such as brakemen and porters, would be filled by African Americans, while conductors and engineers remained white. Southern railroads also facilitated the slave trade by transporting slaves across state borders in freight and baggage cars. Olmsted noted he had "not been on or seen a railroad train, departing southward, that it did not convey a considerable number" of trafficked humans. Slavery is the sleeper over which the nation runs. After the Civil War, some abolitionist politicians argued against Chinese immigration for fear their cheap labor would effectively reinstate the slave system. Southern plantations, seeking to replace the slaves they lost, eagerly sought to recruit Chinese. Spirals or progress or both? Civic life, Olmsted argued, was characterized by conflict and the constant navigation of personal space. Cities in particular created a narrow view of our environment and our interaction with others. This intimacy created by modernity meant we would always look at the world "watchfully, jealously . . . without sympathy." Olmsted's landscapes were meant to counteract this: to give citizens open space to widen their view. Because of his landscapes' renown, Olmsted was commissioned by Leland Stanford to design his future university. The two men fought over the campus design, however, Olmsted insisting on winding paths, open lawns, and a tree museum, Stanford requiring steel and straight lines. The university was conceived of as a memorial to Stanford's son, dead from typhus. In the end, Olmsted bowed out by composing a giant memorial arch; Stanford had Palm Drive run straight to the train station. In 1896, nine years after designing Stanford's campus, Olmsted suffered a severe mental breakdown. He spent his last years in McLean Hospital, a Massachusetts asylum, for whose grounds he submitted a design and plan that were never executed.

Miss Home: "I pick up my life / And take it with me / And I put it down in / ... Any place that is / ... not Dixie," wrote Langston Hughes in his 1949 poem "One-Way Ticket." Hughes's poem is about the Great Migration that occurred between 1916 and 1970, in which poor economic conditions, racial segregation, and violence led to the northern migration of around six million African Americans. Prior to 1916, more than 90% of African Americans in the United States lived in the South; after the Great Migration, nearly half that southern population now lived in the North and West. The train facilitated the Great Migration as well as provided job opportunities, leading to a relative population explosion of Blacks across the West. Rock Springs, Wyoming, for example, was home to the state's largest Black population due to the town's coal mining industry, which served the Union Pacific. During the late 19th century, the Union Pacific Coal Company operated dozens of mines across southeast Wyoming, solidifying its position through wage competition it created by pitting its workers against one another. Black coal miners specifically were brought in as strikebreakers. The train, however, was not the only draw west. In 1908, Charles and Rosetta Speese, along with three of Charles's brothers, one married sister, and their families, settled an entirely Black farming community called Empire in Wyoming near the Nebraskan border. At its peak, Empire housed 65 Black farming families, a church, and a schoolhouse. During this period, Wyoming also endured five lynchings. The closest to Empire occurred in 1913, when Baseman Taylor, a man taken into medical custody at his family's behest on account of psychosis, was unduly restrained by the white Goshen County sheriff, causing head trauma and seizures. Taylor was then taken to a hotel in lieu of any established jail in the new county, where he was shackled to a bed, burned, choked, and beaten, in full view of other prisoners and hotel guests. He died three days later. By 1920, the community had dwindled to 23 residents; the community collapsed by 1930. Such lynchings occurred across the state and other racial lines. On September 2, 1885, white miners in Rock Springs, enraged by the Union Pacific Coal Department's preferential hiring of Chinese who were paid less for their work, murdered at least 28 Chinese miners and injured 15 others, burning their homes and driving the rest out into the desert. The Rock Springs massacre was part of a wave of anti-Chinese violence across the West, much of which could claim its origins in the Wyoming riot. X marks the spot. Langston Hughes's poem is in part about escape, in part about work, in part about the search for a home that has never existed in America. Rock Springs' African American population has significantly dwindled since the late 19th century, declining soon after the Union Pacific began fueling its locomotives not with coal but diesel.

You: A. Philip Randolph (1889–1979) was a civil rights leader and labor union organizer who, in 1925, helped found the Brotherhood of Sleeping Car Porters, a union representing largely African American porters and maids. Randolph was elected to lead the BSCP in part because, unlike other members, he was not employed by the Pullman Company, one of the nation's single largest employers of Black people at the time. George Pullman, who founded the company, hired Black porters almost exclusively, believing that whites would find train travel more luxurious if Black people waited on them, as most white passengers, accustomed to seeing Black people in service, couldn't afford servants in their own homes. In 1928, poor work conditions and low pay on the railroad pushed Randolph to threaten a strike, but the Pullman Company refused to negotiate. Randolph's strike collapsed, in part because Pullman began to hire Filipino porters. This poem adapts select individual oral testimonies from the men and women represented by the BSCP. Some may argue that, if an archive is not readily available to everyone, it should not be used by just anyone. Others might argue, like the novelist Cristina Rivera Garza, that this poetry of appropriated documentation "participate[s] in ending the dominion of what-is-one's-own" by "radically oppos[ing] notions of property and dominion." When a company claims the bodies and livelihoods of its workers, does appropriating their archived voices free them from that particular dominion or chain them to another? "The communication that makes a community is its sharing," Garza writes in "Disappropriation: Writing with and for the Dead." The railroad, from its inception, was conceived of as a unifying, figural community whose own mechanics also exposed the literal limits of these bonds. We share in common though we cannot always see in common. I, too, am a divided author: I interrupt this text with fact. I interrupt it, too, with imagination. What is factual I express within the limits of poetry, while what is poetic I locate within the limits of the real. My poems may be constructions of language then, but they also reveal the uneasy contact between bodies through time. ("You will never," my mother says to me over tea, "truly understand us.") The railroad as metaphor insists we belong to one another through the work of nation-building while the poem insists we belong to one another because we are human. In both cases this link is based on labor, whether of performance and writing, or of money. Perhaps the elegy, too, is labor. And the best laborers, of course, are meant to be invisible. White passengers were said to prefer Black porters because they found them familiar and "happy-go-lucky," unlike Filipinos whom they deemed "strange." "Maybe it isn't outrageous to start imagining books solely or mostly made of acknowledgments pages," Garza writes. For who is it, really, who made the writing of this book possible? Bring the background into foreground, and that is the poem. You may assemble these notes as you like.

Vainly: As the train now allowed women, formerly relegated to the home, to travel long distances, etiquette guides in the 19th century spent a lot of time discussing what a woman should wear and keep on her person on trains, as well as how a man should behave in mixed spaces. In one etiquette book I find these lines: "A true gentleman treats all women with respect, from the commonest mammy to the lady." The railroad was where we codified displays of chivalry, where a Black woman might find, if briefly, some protection and respect. By the late 1870s, however, race became more important than gender in segregating train cars. Black women, in fact, brought the majority of cases against racial segregation on common carriers precisely because of this system of gender deference. They lost. Only one manual I could find, *On Habits and Manners,* took into consideration the specific problems of race on trains. That manual, written by Mary Frances Armstrong for her Black students at Hampton Normal and Agricultural Institute, includes this telling sentence: "Young men, you should protect the womanhood of your race." This advice was not always followed. From Alice Dunbar-Nelson's diaries, *Give Us Each Day:* "At King's Creek car resolved itself into Jim Crow by simple expedient of white passengers moving forward. Fresh white youth wanted me to move out, to the hysterical delight of the colored passengers, who knew me." Did Ida B. Wells read these manuals? In 1883, while traveling by train to Memphis, Wells was asked by the conductor of the Chesapeake, Ohio and Southwestern Railroad Company to give up her seat. This was in direct violation of the 1875 Civil Rights Act, which banned discrimination on the basis of race in theaters, hotels, or transport. Wells, a journalist, suffragist, and antilynching activist, knew her rights. In her autobiography, *Crusade for Justice,* she describes biting the conductor and bracing her feet against the seats until he brought in two other white men to drag her out. When Wells returned to Memphis, she hired a lawyer to sue the railroad, and won. The railroad appealed to the state supreme court, however, which reversed the lower court's decision. Later, Wells, in her diaries, lamented her lack of Victorian feminine virtues, calling herself "tempestuous, rebellious," bemoaning her "disposition to question authority." I don't think her lament can possibly be sincere. When I think of Wells now, I think of a train steaming northward. Beside the line, a sheaf of papers, a train conductor with a ring of teeth marks in his hand.

Face: The stereoscope was invented in 1832 by Sir Charles Wheatstone, though many credit it to the Scottish physicist Sir David Brewster, a rival whose personal contribution to the invention was changing Wheatstone's mirrors out for prisms to unite the two dissimilar pictures into a single 3D image. Andrew J. Russell (1829–1902) was the official US War Department photographer during the Civil War and the official photographer for the Union Pacific Railroad. By 1869, Russell had produced more than 200 glass plate photos and 400 stereo cards of the railroad, the latter objects the Union Pacific sold to investors. The War Department hired Russell to document the effects of battle; the Union Pacific used him to promote the railroad. With one technology, Russell thus unites the machinery of the Civil War with that of the transcontinental. Is war an advertisement? Is the transcontinental martial? The Union Pacific's website currently boasts that Lincoln conceived of the transcontinental as part of the Civil War itself: a way to unite the nation, yes, but foremost as a rail system that could carry war munitions quickly out into the West where Lincoln believed the next civil war would start. Whichever fact you focus on is the story you could tell of this nation. A first glance at Russell's transcontinental photos reveals the project to be inhuman: great cliffs and carapaces of stone, webworks of trestles. Look closer, however, and you spot the humans—clustered, fragile, alone. In my poem, I deliberately get a detail wrong: Russell photographed but never made any stereograph of a dead soldier—that was the work of another artist, Thomas C. Roche. I simply want to draw certain facts closer together. Russell traveled so often that his name does not appear with his wife and two daughters' on any census record except for the year 1860. I do not know if this loss saddened or relieved them or both, as his wife's and daughters' stories are not recorded. I know of their existence only through Russell's biography; in history, they exist because he did. It is only when I peer through a very specific lens that I sense their presences, that I can begin—even faintly—to make their own stories out.

Homeward Facing: *Works and Days* is, at heart, a farmer's almanac in which Hesiod instructs his conniving brother, Perses, to settle down and take care of the family land. Perses had blown through his inheritance and also stripped Hesiod of his own share by bribing the courts to gift him the remaining family farm. *Works and Days* is thus both an admonishment and an attempt at fraternal healing. But Hesiod's poem might also be read as part of the story of Greek colonial expansion and conquest, as a population explosion during the 8th through 6th centuries BCE created land scarcity and anxiety over resources. Through that lens, *Works and Days* is a poem about suffering, strife, and ownership. Strife creates wars, Hesiod warns, and how to heal discord but through work? Lincoln, too, understood the work of the transcontinental to be stitching the nation back together after a war that pitted "brother against brother." And it did not surprise me that during the contentious 2020 election, then–Vice President Joseph Biden proposed a new high-speed rail system that would span the country and allow people to travel across the West in a matter of hours. The train both unites and divides: it is the deepest, purest, most powerful fantasy of America. The work of the railroad is the work of empire, and for America to rise again and again, it must reinvest in its fantasy of itself as renewable, progressive, flexible. We are all servants of empire one way or another; I do not exclude myself in this. The extravagance of this poem I have produced reveals that I, too, am empire's scribe. That in my attempt to critique the achievement I have also celebrated it; that it would be dishonest not to celebrate what inspires, at its root, a kind of wonder. For if I do not choose, also, to commemorate, do I further erase the workers? I refuse to abandon *all* fantasies of my nation. The railroad is built of words as much as steel. I lay down another sleeper.

Terrace: Terrace is one of the most visited ghost towns along the dead transcontinental line, a draw for professional and amateur archeologists alike interested in Chinese workers' artifacts. The day I visited with the state historian, I found shards of old soy sauce bottles, a shirt button, several fragments of an opium pipe. The Chinese section of Terrace is, according to its wreckage, close to what was once the town dump. Even 150 years on, the earth carries evidence of our segregation. Meanwhile, on the phone, a Chinese friend complains to me about another artifact of the transcontinental: Andrew J. Russell's iconic photo *East and West Shaking Hands at Laying Last Rail*. It is not the absence of Chinese in this photo that enrages him, surprisingly, but the fact that Chinese Americans now are outraged at all. "Who cares if they weren't photographed?" he says. "In fact, they were eating a nice lunch at a private party Strobridge threw them." Whether Strobridge served them lunch is not, I say, the point. "And what is the point?" he demands. "Those men invented *nothing,* they owned *nothing.* Their labor was for others with more imagination than them." To work for others, I understand his anger to mean, is shameful. We collect evidence not from the makers of capital but from the owners. My friend owned a San Francisco business that exported consumer products to Mexico; he sold it for a nice profit in 2005. The record is full of capital's owners. Am I an author or an owner, since I leave a material record, and does the presence of other voices in these poems release me from or bind me tighter to the burden of ownership? Institutions have paid me to produce this book. Translation of the Artist into Document. Translation of the Document into Endless Grant Proposal.

Not Fulfill: Leland Stanford, a former lawyer from New York, moved to California in 1852 during the Gold Rush. In 1861, along with Collis Potter Huntington, Mark Hopkins, and Charles Crocker, he established the Central Pacific Railroad, serving as its president. When the Southern Pacific leased and finally stopped CPRR operations in 1885, Stanford remained in power, acting as the Southern Pacific's president until 1890. Stanford also served as governor of California from 1862 to 1863, and as a US senator from 1885 until his death in 1893. In 1876, Stanford and his wife, Jane, purchased a red sandstone mansion in Palo Alto as part of a 650-acre estate they later expanded to 8,000 acres. Many of the workers on this estate were Chinese. The estate was badly damaged in the April 1906 earthquake, which destroyed the main section of the residence. In 1884, Leland, Jr.—their only child—died of typhus; the Stanfords used the wealth they'd planned to gift him to found Stanford University, "to serve the children of California." The campus buildings are composed of locally sourced yellow sandstone and red tile roofs, which were dressed and carved by Italian tradesmen. Everyone leaves a material record. Early in his career, Stanford argued against Chinese immigration, labeling the Chinese an "inferior race." During the transcontinental's construction, he reversed this position and argued it would be beneficial for half a million more Chinese to enter the country. After the railroad was completed, he reverted again, supporting the anti-Chinese Geary Act in 1892. Stanford died in 1893 from heart failure; Jane Stanford died in 1905, poisoned by strychnine. Today, Asian and Asian American students compose 25% of Stanford University.

High Ambition: One of the striking things about Chinese artifacts along the transcontinental line is their uniformity: the same earthenware dishes, the same metal buttons and opium pipes. It suggests the paucity of choice but also the strong connection workers had to their suppliers along the line. But there are other connections Chinese workers developed. Chinese men occasionally intermarried with Indigenous women, as they were imagined by American law to possess similar racial standing. According to the family history of Sandy Lee, a third-generation Chinese Native American, her own great-grandfather Lee Yik-Gim was even captured and adopted by a chief who'd lost his son. Yik-Gim remained with his adopted father for years, Lee said, eventually being elevated to the position of "a minor chief." One orphaned Chinese child named Yong Luung Sing was adopted by Shoshones and renamed "Sharp Eyes." In the absence of Chinese records in the official Central Pacific archives are Paiute and Shoshone oral testimonies. I am struck by how powerfully one culture can carry the memory of another inside it. One man, Wong Sing, became fluent in the Ute language and could rattle off from memory every major event that had happened to the native communities along the line. When he died, 60 Paiute elders assembled before the Indian agent's office to commemorate him. "Elegy" is an insufficient word for the act of sharing grief, this sharing being its own declaration of endurance. I do not know if all these men were outliers to their cultures, or if they expressed through their actions private sentiments not always shared. Regardless, the fragment of history remains a history. In Terrace, when I raise up a cup shard with its British crown stamped on the bottom, the state historian asks, "How does it feel holding a century in your hand?" I remember Po Po telling me as a child how the British-owned shops in Hong Kong had signs reading, *No Chinese or dogs allowed.* I thumb the shard. Even fifty years after leaving China, whenever Po Po or Gung Gung heard the word "British" uttered, they would turn and curse in Cantonese.

Bury: In *Massacre at Duffy's Cut: Tragedy & Conspiracy on the Pennsylvania Railroad,* brothers and authors Drs. William E. Watson and J. Francis Watson argue that the Philadelphia and Columbia Railroad lied about the 1832 cholera-related deaths of 57 Irish railroad workers just outside Philadelphia. They claim it wasn't cholera that killed them but mass murder sparked by panic over cholera. While not a story about the transcontinental, a cholera story is still about the train. Both the Irish and the railroad were blamed for the spread of cholera: the Irish incorrectly, the railroads correctly, as ease of travel made disease transmission more rapid among growing populations. Cholera readjusted our ideas of space and community, just as the railroad changed our ideas of time. Because of the train, phrases such as "time's up," "time's a-wasting," and "the train is leaving the station" entered our vocabulary. The transcontinental led to the division of the nation into four standard time zones to prevent crashes. But if the railway changed our clocks, it also changed our bodies' perception of time. *Railway spine* was a 19th century term for the bodily and psychic disorders that passengers experienced after suffering railway accidents, the result of being hurled through space, propelled into the future. Death, suddenly, seemed everywhere. Like cholera, the train made us uncomfortably aware of our mortal intimacy with each other, which may be why John Palfrey of the Brattle Square Church in Boston delivered this 1832 sermon on cholera, declaring society plagued by corruption, but that it was also through this disease that "[a] merciful God [would] straighten the world out." Such moralizing continues. In 2020, certain environmentalists lauded the COVID-19 pandemic for its influence on climate change, though the World Health Organization estimates that, between January 1, 2020 and December 31, 2021, 14.91 million people had died. Intimacy does not require or necessarily produce empathy. In 1889, a local historian named Julian F. Sachse interviewed a man who swore he'd seen the ghosts of the 57 Irish workers dancing over their mass grave. Sachse suggests the man's memory was faulty; he'd imagined ghosts from the atmospheric lights of ignis fatuus "caused by so many of the Cholera victims being buried together without a sufficient covering of earth; further that the Phenomena was frequently observed on the battle fields during the late rebellion." The man refused to believe it. *I saw what I saw,* he insisted. Sachse's transcript is full of the man's tics and drunken repetitions; it is designed to make us distrust his history. Or maybe that isn't the point. My father, too, during the pandemic, repeated himself, afraid of death, afraid of my death. I would call every day to see if he was healthy. Our cities were in the vise-grip of the pandemic, and now time had expanded to the size of a continent. For two years, all I could hold of him was his voice. *Don't come home,* he'd beg me. Relational time asks if the thing speeding toward us is our past or our future; perhaps because of this, the train itself became a symbol for the movement between consciousness and memory. "Trains of thought are continually passing to and fro, from the light into the dark, and back from the dark into the light," wrote the critic E.S. Dallas in 1867. The railroad workers were murdered in 1832; in August 2004, some were disinterred. So many died. So many have died. I saw what I saw.

Soil: Brigham Young (1801–1877), the second president of the LDS Church and founder of Salt Lake City, was an enthusiastic proponent of the transcontinental but wanted the line to travel through Salt Lake, not Ogden, where the Union Pacific finally routed it. Both General Dodge and Stanford touted the benefits of Young's Mormon workers since, as Dodge reported, they were "teetotalers to the last man, tolerated no gambling, were quiet and law-abiding . . . and concluded each day's labor with communal prayers and songs." But while the railroad companies liked Mormons, they didn't always pay them. Brigham Young, desperate to have the railroad completed to link the Utah Territory to the Pacific, quietly paid the workers himself with church funds, but not without sending furious telegrams to Dodge about the two million dollars owed them. The Union Pacific didn't pay because it had long ago run out of cash and just kept lying about it, though perhaps Dodge also didn't trust Mormons as much as he'd claimed. Travelogues by East Coast journalists visiting the Utah Territory worried over what DC politicians called "The Mormon and Indian Problem," and the 1857 Mormon-led Mountain Meadows massacre of the Baker-Fancher emigrant wagon train in southern Utah had long fed East Coast fantasies of insurrectionist Mormons. Polygamy didn't help. Cartoons in American papers depicted desiccated Mormon men linking hands with women from other polygamous and conspicuously nonwhite cultures, implying that Mormons were racially suspect, un-American. At the heart of all these reports, naturally, was the question of who or what would control the Territory. And who or what are Mormons? (*It's OK to be white*, reads the poster taped up outside my work building.) The Mormons worked the transcontinental line through a grasshopper infestation similar to the cricket infestation that occurred in 1848, which nearly destroyed the crops of the Mormon pioneers before the miraculous arrival of seagulls that devoured all the insects. It's a story, of course. Mostly made up. Just like this letter of Young's that I've composed.

Earth: The 1862 Pacific Railroad Act granted the Central Pacific and Union Pacific aid to construct the railroads and also gave the government use of the line for postal, military, or telegraph services. It ensured the railroads legal right-of-way across the country while giving the railroads possession of all lands within 10 miles on each side of the tracks, exclusive of cities and waterways, which not only allowed the railroads to claim Indigenous territory but even now gives private companies jurisdiction over the lands through which their trains run. If you were to cross within 20 feet of any railroad yard now, security guards—called bulls—would have the legal right to defend it by any means necessary. Freighthoppers I interviewed frequently mentioned the violence of the bulls, the fear of getting caught by men who themselves have no fear of law. One man was beaten so severely he almost lost an eye. Another rider, a woman, was threatened with rape. Today, Havre, Montana, is the most notoriously violent yard in America. The Wild West remains in the space around the railroad, in which you are neither citizen nor subject of the state but of the line itself. *I like to see it lap the miles,* Dickinson wrote. This line travels down the dark, taking you with it. You can never cross the line.

Know: American historian Frederick Jackson Turner (1861–1932) delivered his famous paper "The Significance of the Frontier in American History" in 1893, garnering wide acclaim from historians and other intellectuals. His argument that the American character is forged along the frontier line that separates civilization from wilderness suggests that American culture is not shaped by government incentives and politics but the innate desire to conquer territory. The individualism required and fostered by this conquest accompanies our ideas of democratic freedom itself, leading to an American society inherently suspicious of high culture, religious and political institutions—and finally defined by violence. The frontier line is, in Turner's formation, a distinctly male space that's also white. The frontier divides East and West, Turner argues, the East being a force forever attempting to seize control while the West struggles toward freedom. Of course, this is if you believe only white men sought the frontier. Here are just a scattering of the toponyms you might find on a 19th-century western map: Chinaman Springs, Whorehouse Meadow, China Hat, China Gulch, Jap Valley, Squaw Mountain, Dago Gulch. Many of these names have since been corrected by the US Geological Survey's Domestic Names Committee, which sanitizes place names like Nigger Hill to Negro Hill or Niger. But even on our corrected maps, in 2006 the Geographic Names Information System still listed 60 official toponyms that include the words *Japanese* or *Japan,* 459 that include *Chinese* or *China,* 109 with *Italian* or *Italy,* and 26 with *African* or *Africa.* I understand the desire to alter the map even as some perverse part of me prefers the original. I want the map to reveal all its frontier lines. Another way of saying it: the map's racism, even as it attempts to erase, re-presences. It delineates both spatial and historical time. *History does not move only forward for the American.* Turner's frontier thesis argued that if environment shapes character, we in turn race and acculturate land. Read each point of the map. I, too, settle this country with my blood and time.

Your: Sir Richard Francis Burton (1821–1890) was a British writer, linguist, cartographer, ethnographer, poet, diplomat, soldier, spy and translator. Fluent in 29 languages, Burton was perhaps most renowned for making a pilgrimage to Mecca disguised as a Persian mirza and, later, a Sunni dervish, and also for his unexpurgated English translation of *One Thousand and One Nights.* Burton cultivated a scandalous reputation based in part on his interest in erotic literature and the frankness with which he wrote about the sexual practices of the cultures he studied. Considering Burton's curiosity about sex, it is perhaps no surprise he was drawn to the Utah Territory, as it is impossible to think about Mormons without also considering polygamy. In Utah, sex and statehood go hand in hand. While the United States did not nationally legalize women's suffrage until 1920, western territories did so to bolster conservative voting blocks; the Utah Territory in particular was considered by East Coast activists as a testing ground for women's suffrage, since the hope was that Mormon women would vote polygamy out, thus demonstrating that suffrage could give women a voice different from their husbands' and fathers'. Polygamy, however, was never on any Utah referendum. When Utah women didn't vote out polygamy, Congress passed the 1887 Edmunds-Tucker Act, punitively stripping them of their voting rights. Furious, Utah women lobbied for re-enfranchisement and, when Utah became a state in 1896, it entered the union with women's voting rights intact. In 1890, the LDS Church officially renounced polygamy, not out of interest for its women, but because it faced federal confiscation of its temples. All this is history, but Burton wasn't interested in suffrage: he wanted to know if Mormon women were pretty. Throughout his book *The City of the Saints,* he seems continually chagrinned by my state's general lack of eroticism. It's a thought I've had myself, having met both polygamous and polyamorous couples here, struck by their oddly perfunctory, even insular nature. Perhaps when you have so openly expanded your territory, you must attend it more closely? Or perhaps it's because some men in my own family were known to be polygamous: a wife in China, a wife in America. Regardless, I am bored as Burton here, where sex lives are reduced to the language of corporations. *We are each partners in this union.* Perhaps I'm bored by erotic speculation itself, having walked as a child between my mother and father, watching strangers watch our bodies, imagining the act that linked us, one to the other. Sex is one of the primary ways we are nationed, raced. Through our bodies, your eyes remind me, we can make Americans of anyone.

Heroic: Helen Holmes (1892–1950) was an American silent-movie actress famous for her originating role in *The Hazards of Helen*, a western adventure series of 119 twelve-minute films that feature Helen, a telegrapher, foiling the plots of dastardly men. *The Hazards of Helen* was not the only film series about plucky young women surviving life in the West: there were also *The Perils of Pauline*, and the Ruth Roland serials *Ruth of the Rockies* and *The Timber Queen*. *The Hazards of Helen* was produced by the Kalem Company specifically to compete with *The Perils of Pauline* serial, which, unlike Holmes's films, featured a female protagonist perpetually in distress. Helen, in contrast, single-handedly overcomes all criminals and calamities. In *The Girl and the Game* serial alone, Helen saves her boyfriend and father from a train wreck, saves the railroad from financial ruin, recovers the train's payroll from thieves, rescues another male character from a lynching, captures more thieves while also saving two men from a mine cave-in, and finally uncouples a freight train to prevent a crash. It is exhausting to watch. Holmes, like her film character, was a railroader's daughter who grew up around trains and, like Ruth Roland, performed her own stunts. The Helen Holmes and Ruth Roland films were extremely popular with men, but they were designed to attract a growing female audience, one that had evolved with a changing nation and burgeoning Hollywood culture. Prior to the 20th century, westward migration in America was largely male; by 1900, however, female western migrants outpaced male ones. By the time of the booming nickelodeon business between 1905 and 1914, movies had begun to focus on women in the West, in particular in Los Angeles, a city publicists characterized as where "the Occident and the Orient" finally met. I doubt my great-grandmother Ethel watched these films, as she disliked movies, though she herself was the first female telegrapher and shipwright in Seattle. And Po Po would also have disdained them, though at age 18 she'd rescued her own sister from an abusive marriage. From what I remember, these stoic, exceptional women never met. I suspect if they had, they would have understood each other. Each possessed a similar outlook on gender and life, specifically the belief that, though women worked harder than men, sons were more valuable. Po Po eventually even transferred her preference for men onto my father, despite his being white. I remember the 80th birthday party my mother threw for her and how, after opening every present my mother had bought, Po Po would turn and thank my father extravagantly. I do not know why the women in my family so willingly discounted the strength of others like them, or whether they truly had so little respect for their own accomplishments. Perhaps it was a form of modesty; more likely it was learned self-hatred. Despite its persistence in popular culture, the ubiquity of the silent-film trope of a helpless woman tied to the tracks is largely fantasy: the two such images that exist were in comedies. Holmes herself paid ironic homage to the trope in her serial *A Lass of the Lumberlands,* in which she rescues her hapless boyfriend, Tom, roped and left sprawled like a calf across the track irons.

Heart: Scottish novelist and poet Robert Louis Stevenson (1850–1894) published *Across the Plains with Other Memories and Essays* in 1892. It is the second installment of his three-part American travel memoir that begins with *The Amateur Emigrant* and concludes with *Silverado Squatters,* a trio of books that might be considered Stevenson's love story, as they were occasioned by his travels across the US to join his American lover, Fanny Van de Grift Osbourne, and her children in San Francisco. I suppose this book, too, is a love story. After the Trump presidency, after the insurrection, after the rounds of protests and counterprotests, after the first and second then third wave of the pandemic, after my mother refused out of fear to shop in Chinatown, after a Filipina my mother's age was punched and kicked on video by a stranger in New York, do I believe still in the promise of this union? As reports of anti-Asian violence mounted, my mother retreated into her house, and I avoided the news, embarrassed. The pandemic and its effects exposed a lingering rift in our family: unlike my mother and cousins, I hide in plain sight. In truth, I've felt this rift since Gung Gung's death, a fracturing that only deepened after the loss of Po Po. While my grandparents were alive, my mother could see herself in them; without them, she began to pull away from other family members, including myself. Always easy to anger, now she lashed out more quickly, disappointed perhaps by how I reminded her of the ways that, over time, she has failed to remain Chinese. Po Po had always loved my mother and me in a distant way, preferring her sons and my more Asian-looking cousins. Gung Gung, for whatever reason, seemed to prefer my mother and me, perhaps because he loved this nation more than Po Po did, more than my mother and I could. I long to feel about America as Gung Gung did. I look in the mirror and nothing like him looks back. *Why don't you come home?* my mother asks, surprised that I've never returned to Seattle. But here, living 100 miles away from the dead transcontinental, I feel something in me open. What my mother said has come true. I am now more comfortable in the West than with her.

Dead: If the transcontinental was meant, finally, to draw America closer to China, it failed. The transcontinental facilitated trade between the coasts and helped shape a national cultural life, but it did not increase American trade to China. Likewise, if the transcontinental was meant to lower travel costs for passengers, that too failed. The cost of a sleeper car from Chicago to Sacramento now runs you close to six thousand dollars. Trains traveling to Sacramento are largely empty of passengers, loaded instead with cars, appliances, crates of olive oil, military vehicles, nuclear waste. The train, imagined as an international event, turned us insular. Perhaps the most significant, and accidental, benefit was for hobos migrating during the Great Depression. Riders, as they call themselves, are rare now because of the cheapness of Greyhound and the ubiquity of the car. Riders jump container cars when trains stop for off-loading. They hide in a container's front and rear in spaces that can fit two at a time to sleep, though the open-air exposure means riders have to wear bandannas to keep their chapped lips from bleeding. Riders track safe jumping times with the aid of a xeroxed crew-change guide that, according to the riders, must never be shared with outsiders. When I asked one rider why he did it, he said he didn't know. Most people who jump trains are young, white, middle-class. They take aliases on the rails and tend to avoid each other. Another rider I spoke to said they're attracted to the anonymity and the lawlessness. To ride the rails, he told me, you need to like being invisible. After a few hours in the open air listening to the cars rock beneath you, you start hearing shrieks and voices. The sound moves through your body, the world a scream you can't turn off. It's as close as he's ever come to an extended hallucination. Maybe that's why the riders you meet are mostly ex-military, he said. The exposure, the noise, the motion—it sends you out of body, out of time. One guy returned from Afghanistan said it was the only thing that could relax him. He said it was the closest thing to being in a war.

Not Ash: Sui Sin Far (1865–1914), born Edith Maude Eaton, was a journalist and fiction writer, the daughter of an English merchant, Edward Eaton, and a Chinese mother, Achuen Grace Amoy, whom Eaton met on a business trip to Shanghai. Far worked for a variety of Canadian and American publications, largely writing about the Chinese communities she encountered on her travels. I do not know what, in real life, her relationship was like with her mother, a former slave who as a child worked as an acrobat and tightrope dancer for a Chinese company before being rescued by missionaries. Far's Cantonese pen name and her stories focusing on Chinese life in the West, however, suggest she saw something of her deepest self reflected in her mother; that, though she could have, she preferred never to pass as white. I first read Far's personal essay "Leaves from the Mental Portfolio of a Eurasian" just after graduate school. The memories she'd had of racially disguising herself, then of refusing to be disguised, felt distressingly familiar. One anecdote she relates, of being trapped in a room with a British naval officer who insists she succumb to his advances, made me feel, briefly, like I suffered from vertigo. The essay was written in Seattle and published in 1909. One can say *echoes*. One can say *similarities,* and one can argue that the insistence on these similarities obscures. The English poem reflects the Chinese, but it is not the Chinese poem. The past is not simply a translation of the present. I can say that at times I feel like Far or that I look like my mother, but my life is different from theirs. We are citizens of different countries. The slap in my relationship with my mother is agreeing that some part of me will never be her daughter. In me, she loses what she's already lost: father, mother, language, culture. Of course, she and I ignore this, pretending that the divisions I've learned to contain within myself don't become unbridgeable when I'm with her. What draws us together holds us apart. I don't think there is a language adequate to express this break at our center, even as my awareness of it helps me see my mother with more sympathy. Perhaps this is about race, perhaps not. But race has certainly made our private experiences more private. Sui Sin Far's name in Cantonese means "narcissus flower." My Chinese name I refuse to translate. *I love you. I believe that. It's OK to be* _____.

Translation: Over the course of this book, I have taken the literal meanings Dr. Wu has translated for me to produce what is a most likely, if not always accurate, outcome. I know my English titles are poor renditions of his Chinese, at once too strict and wildly erratic. Scholars will disagree with my translation; I do not know Chinese. And since so few people in my family speak it, I know that I will never learn. My family's loss of language means my own exclusion from their past. Does this matter? And does it matter I haven't shared the other poem with you here, the second half of that pair carved into the walls of Angel Island? I haven't told you what characters comprise that poem, and though I know it's been translated as its own work, I don't know whether the Chinese would allow me to read across both poems' lines, stitching them together so that the sense of one bleeds into the other. Perhaps the poems are only complete when read this way. Perhaps each should stand alone. I suspect both. Regardless, the subject of both poems is the same: the loss, the striving, the hope, the death that is startling and continuous. Perhaps, having read only one poem, you long to see the other. Start over. Grief is but one moment of time. The elegy goes on forever.

Bibliography

Stephen E. Ambrose, *Nothing Like It in the World: The Men Who Built the Transcontinental Railroad 1863–1869*, 2001.

Mary Frances Armstrong, *On Habits and Manners*, 1888.

David Haward Bain, *Empire Express: Building the First Transcontinental Railroad*, 1999.

Samuel Bowles, *Across the Continent: A Summer's Journey to the Rocky Mountains, the Mormons, and the Pacific States with Speaker Colfax*, 1865.

Sir Richard Francis Burton, *The City of the Saints: Among the Mormons and Across the Rocky Mountains to California*, 1861.

Gordon H. Chang and Shelley Fisher Fishkin, eds, *The Chinese and the Iron Road: Building the Transcontinental Railroad*, 2014.

Sue Fawn Chung and Priscilla Wegars, eds, *Chinese American Death Rituals: Respecting the Ancestors*, 2005.

Jeanne Fogle Cook, *Experiences of Orphan Train Riders: Implications for Child Welfare Policy*, dissertation, University of South Carolina, 1994.

Iyko Day, *Alien Capital: Asian Racialization and the Logic of Settler Colonial Capitalism*, 2016.

Sarah Del Seronde, *Metal Road: A Day in the Life of a Navajo Railroader*, 2017.

Hilary A. Hallett, *Go West, Young Women! The Rise of Early Hollywood*, 2013.

Florence Hartley, *The Ladies' Book of Etiquette, and Manual of Politeness*, 1860.

Lucie Cheng Hirata, "Free, Indentured, Enslaved: Chinese Prostitutes in Nineteenth Century America," *Signs: Journal of Women in Culture and Society*, Vol. 5, No. 1, 1979, 3–29.

Walter R. Houghton and others, *American Etiquette and Rules of Politeness*, 1889.

Manu Karuka, *Empire's Tracks: Indigenous Nations, Chinese Workers, and the Transcontinental Railroad*, 2019.

Dennis Kearney, *Speeches of Dennis Kearney, Labor Champion*, 1878.

Theodore Kornweibel, Jr., *Railroads in the African American Experience: A Photographic Journey*, 2010.

Him Mark Lai, Genny Lim, Judy Yung, *Island: Poetry and History of Chinese Immigrants on Angel Island, 1910–1940*, 1980.

Brigham D. Madsen, *Corinne: The Gentile Capital of Utah*, 1980.

Mark Monmonier, *From Squaw Tit to Whorehouse Meadow: How Maps Name, Claim, and Inflame*, 2006.

National Orphan Train Complex website (orphantraindepot.org).

Frederick Law Olmsted, *A Journey in the Seaboard Slave States, with Remarks on Their Economy*, 1856.

Patricia Ann Pawlak, *The Diary of Mary McKeon, an Irish American Domestic Servant in Nineteenth Century America*, Duke University MA thesis, 2016.

Amy G. Richter, *Home on the Rails: Women, the Railroads and the Rise of Public Domesticity*, 2005.

Michael Rutter, *Upstairs Girls: Prostitution in the American West*, 2012.

Alex Ruuska, "Ghost Dancing and the Iron Horse: Surviving Through Tradition and Technology," *Technology and Culture*, July 2011, Vol. 52, 574–97.

Wong Sam and assistants, *An English-Chinese Phrase Book*, 1875.

Stephanie J. Shaw, *What A Woman Ought to Be and Do: Black Professional Women Workers During the Jim Crow Era*, 1996.

T.L. Stedman and K.P. Lee, *A Chinese and English Phrase Book in the Canton Dialect, or Dialogues on Ordinary and Familiar Subjects*, 1888.

Robert Louis Stevenson, *Across the Plains with Other Memories and Essays*, 1892.

Henry David Thoreau, *Walden, or Life in the Woods*, 1854.

Anthony Trollope, *North America*, 1862.

Frederick Jackson Turner, *The Frontier in American History*, 1920.

Richard White, *Railroaded: The Transcontinentals and the Making of Modern America*, 2011.

Glenn Willumson, *Iron Muse: Photographing the Transcontinental Railroad*, 2013.

Jay Youngdahl, *Working on the Railroad, Walking in Beauty: Navajo, Hózhǫ́, the Railroad and Track Work*, 2011.

Image Credits

p. 2   Andrew J. Russell, *East and West Shaking Hands at Laying Last Rail,* Beinecke Rare Book and Manuscript Library, Yale University.

p. 45   Andrew J. Russell, *Shoshone Indians,* Beinecke Rare Book and Manuscript Library, Yale University.

p. 50   *Carlisle Indian Industrial School,* Pennsylvania, ca 1900. Public domain.

p. 56   Jack Delano, *Clovis, New Mexico. Women employed at the Atchison, Topeka and Santa Fe Railroad yard to clean out the potash jars. Left to right: Almeta Williams, Beatrice Davis, Liza Goss, and Abbie Caldwell,* Farm Security Administration/ Office of War Information Collection, Library of Congress, 1943.

p. 65   *A Chinese prostitute looking out the window of a crib door, Chinatown, San Francisco,* from R.D. Miller, *Shady Ladies of the West,* Westernlore Press, Los Angeles, CA, 1964.

p. 89   Andrew J. Russell, *Hall's Fill above Granite Canon,* Beinecke Rare Book and Manuscript Library, Yale University.

p. 95   T.C. Roche, *Dead Confederate Soldier in the Trenches,* Library of Congress.

p. 106 *Winslow, Arizona. A young Indian laborer working in the Atchison, Topeka and Santa Fe Railroad yard,* Farm Security Administration/Office of War Information Collection, Library of Congress.

p. 112 Helen Holmes in a film still from *Lass of the Lumberlands,* 1916.

p. 124 Mike Call, photo of *Spiral Jetty.*

p. 172 Joel Long, tundra swans.

Speakers

The poems "Wrap" and "You" are adapted from archival letters and oral-history transcriptions available online.

"Wrap" draws on letter transcripts at "Immigrant Letters," the Irish Portal, Provincial Archives of New Brunswick, unless otherwise noted. Also consulted was "Irish Immigrant Letters Home," Historical Society of Pennsylvania. The Mary McKeon diary is transcribed in Patricia Ann Pawlak's MA thesis referenced in the bibliography.

1. Jane and James MacKintosh to Margaret, 1858
2. Patrick O'Neill to his brother John O'Neill, 1868, from "Letters of Irish Immigrants," Carlow County, Ireland Genealogy Projects
3. John Browne to Michael Studdart, 1849

4. Mary McKeon diary
5. Catherine Hennagan to her father and mother, 1848
6. Lewis Doyle to John Doyle, 1873, as quoted in Malcolm Campbell, *Ireland's New Worlds*
7. Ference McGowan to his parents, 1847
8. J. Nugent (undated fragment)
9. unknown cousin to John McCarthy, 1903, and Cousin Josephine to John McCarthy, no date
10. Mrs. Jas. McCarthy to Edward McCarthy, 1888
11. Samuel Gilman to his wife, 1849, Maine Historical Society, Maine Memory Network
12. unknown cousin to John McCarthy, 1903
13. John Browne to Michael Studdart, 1849
14. Mary McKeon diary

"You" draws from "Robert C. Hayden: Transcripts of oral history interviews with Boston African American Railroad Workers, 1977–91," at the Joseph P. Healey Library, University of Massachusetts Boston. The interviews referenced occurred in 1988 and 1989.

Epigraph: Albert Floyd, Flake

1. Albert Floyd Flake
2. Willard M. Chandler
3. Overton Wesley Crawford and Alfred Floyd Flake
4. Richmond Belcher
5. Chico Holmes
6. Albert Floyd Flake
7. Mann Coley Mayo and Willard M. Chandler
8. Richmond Belcher
9. Frances E. Rideout
10. Chorus
11. Chico Holmes
12. Chico Holmes
13. Chorus

Acknowledgments

Thank you to Judge Michael Kwan and the Chinese Railroad Workers Descendants Association, the Utah State Historical Preservation Office, the University of Utah Confucius Institute and Dr. Fusheng Wu, the Utah State Historic Preservation Office and Dr. Christopher Merritt, and Max Chang and the Spike 150 Foundation. Thanks also to Everett Bassett, Matt Basso, Joelle Biele, Jaimi Butler, Kai Carlson-Wee, Jimmy Chen, Ling-Ling Chen, Richard Cheu, Ava Chin, Baldwin Chiu, Ada Con, Sarah Del Seronde, Paul Edwards, Joan Naviyuk Kane, Summer Mei Ling Lee, David Lei, Hilton Obenzinger, Kim Ornellas, Monty Paret, Marianna Di Paolo, Patrick Phillips, Michael Sheehan, Anthony Shirley, Greg Smoak, Peter Sum, and Sherman Tang. Thanks to Lisa Bickmore, Kimberly Johnson, Natasha Sajé, Susan Sample, and Jennifer Tonge. Thanks, eternally, to Melanie Rae Thon. Thanks to my father and mother. Thanks to the Kan family.

Thanks to the translators I worked with, including Elwood Mose, Tess Whitty, Silvia Creminelli, Royce Spilker, Oscar M. Underwood, Jim Green, and Ben Black Bear.

Thanks also to the editors who published the following poems:

The Academy of American Poets Poem-a-Day: "Have Knowledge," "What Day"

Kenyon Review: "Bury," "Earth," "Homeward Facing" (as "Home-Gazing"), "Know," "Soil"

The Margins: "Body," "Hold Sorrow," "Indeed," "Journey," "Miss Home," "Regret," "Return," "Sorrowful News"

The Map of Every Lilac Leaf: Poets Respond to the Smith College Museum of Art: "Lament" (as "Rolling Power")

Thank you to Michael Wiegers, Claretta Holsey, and Phil Kovacevich at Copper Canyon for producing a beautiful book, and for taking the time to talk through this project's complexities. An extra-special thank you to Jessica Roeder for her heroic and thorough fact-checking. Any mistakes are mine alone.

West is also a website that can be accessed at www.westtrain.org. The video poems were composed with the direction and advice of Jennilyn Merten of Perpendicular Projects. Video footage of the transcontinental was shot by Mike Call. Enormous thanks to Mike, Jennilyn, and to Gwyn Fisher and AgaveWeb for helping design the site.

About the Author

Paisley Rekdal is the author of over ten books of poetry and nonfiction, most recently *Nightingale: Poems* (Copper Canyon Press, 2019) and *Appropriate: A Provocation* (W.W. Norton, 2021). A two-time finalist for the Kingsley Tufts Prize, her work has garnered fellowships from the NEA, the Fulbright Foundation, and the Guggenheim Foundation. She guest-edited *The Best American Poetry 2020,* and her own work is forthcoming from or has appeared in *The New Yorker, American Poetry Review, The New Republic, Poetry, Kenyon Review,* and *The New York Times.* From 2017–2022, she served as Utah's Poet Laureate. She is a distinguished professor of literature at the University of Utah.

Lannan Literary Selections

For two decades Lannan Foundation has supported the publication and distribution of exceptional literary works. Copper Canyon Press gratefully acknowledges their support.

LANNAN LITERARY SELECTIONS 2023

Jaswinder Bolina, *English as a Second Language*

Natalie Eilbert, *Overland*

Amanda Gunn, *Things I Didn't Do with This Body*

Paisley Rekdal, *West: A Translation*

Michael Wiegers (ed.), *A House Called Tomorrow: Fifty Years of Poetry from Copper Canyon Press*

RECENT LANNAN LITERARY SELECTIONS FROM COPPER CANYON PRESS

Chris Abani, *Smoking the Bible*

Mark Bibbins, *13th Balloon*

Jericho Brown, *The Tradition*

Victoria Chang, *Obit*

Victoria Chang, *The Trees Witness Everything*

Leila Chatti, *Deluge*

Shangyang Fang, *Burying the Mountain*

Nicholas Goodly, *Black Swim*

June Jordan, *The Essential June Jordan*

Laura Kasischke, *Lightning Falls in Love*

Deborah Landau, *Soft Targets*

Dana Levin, *Now Do You Know Where You Are*

Philip Metres, *Shrapnel Maps*

Paisley Rekdal, *Nightingale*

Natalie Scenters-Zapico, *Lima :: Limón*

Natalie Shapero, *Popular Longing*

Arthur Sze, *The Glass Constellation: New and Collected Poems*

Fernando Valverde, *America* (translated by Carolyn Forché)

Michael Wasson, *Swallowed Light*

Matthew Zapruder, *Father's Day*

Poetry is vital to language and living. Since 1972, Copper Canyon Press has published extraordinary poetry from around the world to engage the imaginations and intellects of readers, writers, booksellers, librarians, teachers, students, and donors.

WE ARE GRATEFUL FOR THE MAJOR SUPPORT PROVIDED BY:

THE PAUL G. ALLEN
FAMILY FOUNDATION

CULTURE

Lannan

WASHINGTON STATE
ARTS COMMISSION

The Witter Bynner Foundation
for Poetry

TO LEARN MORE ABOUT UNDERWRITING
COPPER CANYON PRESS TITLES,
PLEASE CALL 360-385-4925 EXT. 103

WE ARE GRATEFUL FOR THE MAJOR SUPPORT PROVIDED BY:

Richard Andrews and Colleen
    Chartier
Anonymous
Jill Baker and Jeffrey Bishop
Anne and Geoffrey Barker
Donna Bellew
Matthew Bellew
Sarah Bird
Will Blythe
John Branch
Diana Broze
Sarah Cavanaugh
Keith Cowan and Linda Walsh
Stephanie Ellis-Smith and
    Douglas Smith
Mimi Gardner Gates
Gull Industries Inc. on behalf of
    William True
The Trust of Warren A. Gummow
William R. Hearst III
Carolyn and Robert Hedin
David and Jane Hibbard
Bruce S. Kahn
Phil Kovacevich and Eric Wechsler
Lakeside Industries Inc. on behalf
    of Jeanne Marie Lee

Maureen Lee and Mark Busto
Peter Lewis and Johanna Turiano
Ellie Mathews and Carl Youngmann
    as The North Press
Larry Mawby and Lois Bahle
Hank and Liesel Meijer
Jack Nicholson
Petunia Charitable Fund and
    adviser Elizabeth Hebert
Madelyn Pitts
Suzanne Rapp and Mark Hamilton
Adam and Lynn Rauch
Emily and Dan Raymond
Joseph C. Roberts
Jill and Bill Ruckelshaus
Cynthia Sears
Kim and Jeff Seely
Nora Hutton Shepard
D.D. Wigley
Joan F. Woods
Barbara and Charles Wright
In honor of C.D. Wright,
    from Forrest Gander
Caleb Young as C. Young Creative
The dedicated interns and faithful
    volunteers of Copper Canyon Press

The pressmark for Copper Canyon Press
suggests entrance, connection, and interaction
while holding at its center
an attentive, dynamic space for poetry.

This book is set in Arno Pro and Superclarendon.
Book design by Phil Kovacevich.
Printed in Canada on archival-quality paper.